The Laureate of Gloucestershire

Linns M. Lysakowska
Cambridge
2007

THE LAUREATE OF
GLOUCESTERSHIRE

THE LIFE AND WORK OF
F. W. HARVEY
1888-1957

FRANCES TOWNSEND

REDCLIFFE
Bristol

First published in 1988
by Redcliffe Press Ltd.,
49 Park St., Bristol.

ISBN 0 948265 67 1

The main text in this book has
been set in Garamond 11/12 to a measure of 27 ems.

Photoset, printed and bound by
WBC Bristol and Maesteg

Contents

Acknowledgements

My special thanks are due to Cecil and Melville Watts and Kerry Counsell who have helped to make the publication of this book possible. The author and the publisher are grateful to F.W. Harvey's son, Mr Patrick Harvey, for permission to quote from his father's work.

Thanks and acknowledgements are due to the following:

Mr F.W. Harvey, Mr Patrick Harvey, Mrs Eileen Griffiths, Mr Brian Frith, Mr Brian Waters, Mr & Mrs A. James, Mr Glyn James, Mr & Mrs L. Baber, Herbert Howells, Mrs I. Woodward, Mrs J. Voyce, Mr Peter Bennett, Dr W. Tandy, Mr Tom Voyce, Mr Vernon Jones, Mrs Gwen Greenish, Mrs Frances Maxwell, Mrs M. Jordan, Miss Hilary Leeds, Mr Robert Waller, Mr Roland Pepper, Mr H. Jarrett, Mrs M. Akers, Mr W. Hatton, Miss I. Harvey, Mrs G. Dye, Mr Arthur Robbins, Mr Frank Green, Mrs Male, Mr A.G. Prosser, W.B. Cornock, Mr Dawson, Mr I. Adams, Mr R. Boo, Mrs S. Mitchell, Miss S. Beaton, Revd S.P. Venables, Lt Col (Retd) H.L.T. Radice MBE, Douglas McLean, The Forest Bookshop, Oxford University Press, Sidgwick & Jackson, Stainer & Bell Ltd, Trustees of the Ivor Gurney Literary Estate, Gloucestershire County Archivist, Gloucester City Library and Gloucester Folk Museum.

Illustrations

Introduction

There are some men who, from the moment of their birth, seem destined for success and fame; who, as the result of good fortune, or their own self-recognition, are able to reach the heights from which their brilliance shines out over lesser men. Yet others, of equal brilliance, are only aware of some intangible difference between them and their fellows, of some restless burning within, which seeks to express itself in a tangible form. Their flame burns brightly for a time, and then exhausts itself.

Such a person was F.W. Harvey, the Gloucestershire poet; a man of great charm and intellect, a brilliant talker with a voice which held his listeners spellbound. He had a gentleness, humour and compassion for his fellows which contrasted with his intense, exclusive love of the county of Gloucestershire, and an almost destructive carelessness for self-interest, with an impractical streak which bordered on irresponsibility.

In his self-portrait Harvey drew a very accurate picture of himself, a man with no practical purpose in life, unassuming, and careless of appearance.

F.W.H.
(A Portrait)

A thick-set, dark-haired, dreamy little man,
    Uncouth to see,
Revolving ever this preposterous plan —
Within a web of words spread cunningly
To tangle Life — no less,
(Could he expect success!)

Of Life, he craves not much, expect to watch.
    Being forced to act,
He walks behind himself, as if to catch
The motive: — an accessory to the fact,
Faintly amused, it seems,
Behind his dreams.[1]

---

[1] From *A Gloucestershire Lad*, Sidgwick & Jackson, 1918, p. 50.

7

Harvey did not seek fame, his only ambition was to be known as Will Harvey — poet. In his lifetime this ambition was achieved mainly within the borders of the county of his birth. His modesty and lack of drive and in later years his withdrawal into himself, prevented his work from reaching a much wider audience. Yet he left behind him much that is worthy of study, and the memories of those who knew him were of a man who was a victim of his sensitivity and idealism.

Childhood and Youth

Frederick William Harvey was born on 26th March, 1888 at Murrel's End, Hartpury, within sight of the tower of Gloucester Cathedral. He was the eldest of five children born to Howard and Cecilia (Tillie) Harvey and he recorded his entry into the world in the following four lines:

> March winds bugled that morn
> In ear of a babe unborn:
> "Up, child! March!"
> Lord, I have heeded Thy horn.[1]

In a letter to someone called Clarke in 1921 he wrote: "The old adage that 'misfortunes never come singly' is justified by the fact that he [FWH] and the rent became due on successive days."[2]

Will, as he became known, was born into a family of horse breeders and dealers, particularly of large horses for brewers' drays, farm horses, and pit ponies for the mines in the Forest of Dean. Will's grandfather was an astute businessman. In the late 1870's and early 1880's there had been three years' drought followed by three years' flood and most of the farmers were tenants who often could not afford to pay their rents, let alone to buy more horses when their own became too old to work. Fred Harvey could see that there was money to be made in horse-breeding and dealing, so he started to buy up young, unbroken Shire horses at the fairs for twenty pounds or so and supplied them in pairs to the local farmers. In return for using the horses free of charge, they broke them in, shod them and fed them and after a couple of years they were replaced by two more, while the original pair would be sold for eighty pounds or more at Gloucester Market.

Not all the Harveys shared Frederick's flair for business. One of his brothers had no success with his farming affairs and by contrast his farm became run down and overgrown. Fred finally took him under his wing and offered him a home and work on his own farm, but he was a loner and a dreamer, preferring to sleep in the hayloft and to drift

---

[1] "26.3.1888", *Gloucestershire*, Oliver & Boyd, 1947, p. 1.
[2] Harvey's Scrapbook, County Record Office, Gloucester.

through life with no cares and responsibilities. This lack of interest in material things, and in striving for society's accepted idea of success in life, was to show itself again later in his great-nephew, Will.

Fortunately for Frederick, his son Howard, Will's father, inherited his father's business acumen and when he eventually took over the farm it continued to flourish.

When Will was two years old, the family moved to a fine, Georgian house called The Redlands at Minsterworth alongside the Severn and it was here that he spent his childhood and youth.

The village was only four miles from Gloucester and was bounded by water to the north and the south and in the years that he spent here, Will became intimate with this stretch of the Severn Vale, with its orchards and lush meadows bordering the river. He grew to know every mood and whim of that tidal stream which could one day be smooth and glittering and the next, boiling and raging, relentlessly sweeping all before it.

The river had long been an important means of transport and communication. Will loved to stand on its bank, watching the salmon fishers, or to get into a boat and explore up or downstream, and Minsterworth was one of the best places from which to view the Severn Bore. In Will's youth the river banks were kept in good order by tenant farmers and landlords, who planted withies along them.

It was not long before his carefree and independent nature began to show itself. He once recalled, "I was a spoilt child, full of faith. At the age of two I tried to walk upon water and discovered I was not Jesus Christ." At about the same time it was one day discovered that he was missing. All the farm labourers and servant girls were sent out to search for him and he was eventually found in the stable, hanging on to the hind leg of one of the most evil-tempered horses on the farm.

Will's father, Howard Harvey, was a short, dark, man, passionately fond of his horses and he tried to pass on his enthusiasm to his sons. When Will was a small boy, learning to ride, he would often complain to his father that his legs ached, but he was simply told, "Then get on and ride again." In the springtime riding horses was even harder, for often the fields and orchards on Severnside were flooded and then the water would reach as high as the ponies' bellies.

Will was short and dark like his father, while his three younger brothers were tall, so he became known affectionately as "the little man".

As his father was so much occupied with the running of the farm, it was Will's mother who had the greatest influence on him and seemed to understand him best. A deep bond grew up between them which later in life may, to a certain extent, have hampered his progress, for she seemed to be aware of his weaknesses and he of her strength, on which he knew he could always rely:

> Once, I remember, when we were at home
> I had come into church, and waited late,
> Ere lastly kneeling to communicate
> Alone: and thinking that you would not come.
>
> Then, with closed eyes (having received the Host)
> I prayed for your dear self, and turned to rise;
> When lo! beside me like a blessed ghost —
> Nay, a grave sunbeam — *you*! Scarcely my eyes
> Could credit it, so softly had you come
> Beside me as I thought I walked alone.[1]

Mrs Harvey realised that Will had an independent streak and probably hoped that the background of a well-ordered family life would eventually train him in self-discipline; but she had not allowed for the abundance of natural charm which he possessed, which compensated for any faults which he might have. Nevertheless, consciously or subconsciously, he was aware of his mother's influence and his desire for her approval right up to the time of her death.

Mrs Harvey was a tall, stately woman, much respected in the village. When one of her sisters-in-law died, leaving the husband with a young daughter to raise, Mrs Harvey took her into her own family to be a companion to her daughter, Gladys, and so the niece remained with them until she married.

In spite of her preoccupation with the farm and six children, Mrs Harvey always found time to help the less fortunate. The poor people of the village called her The Walking Angel of Minsterworth and she became renowned for her sympathy, good work and godliness. She read her Bible and said psalms daily and with her family attended church regularly.

She appointed a Miss Whitehead, the daughter of a clergyman, to be Will's governess, and it was she who taught him to memorise the psalms and to learn poetry. At the age of seven he could recite Shelley's "Skylark" and at the age of eight he knew the whole of "The Pied Piper". At about the same time he was writing poetry in imitation of Longfellow. He always had a great love and appreciation of beauty and he said it was Richard Jefferies who taught him to look around him.

In 1897, at the age of nine, he was sent to The King's School at

---

[1] "The Bond", *Gloucestershire Friends*, Sidgwick & Jackson, 1917, p. 21.

Gloucester, and there, he later claimed, he learned to love music and also *how* to learn. He grew to love the cathedral which was known in the surrounding area as The Sentinel of the Vale and which could be seen clearly from Minsterworth.

As soon as Will came home from school however, his lively imagination was given rein in escapades in which he was frequently the instigator. There were often visits to his cousins, the Babers, whose father kept pigs. Will's uncle had made a strict rule that no-one was to go through the field where the sows were kept, particularly when the boar was there. However, the field was a short cut to the river and one day Will led the others across. Suddenly the boar gave chase. The gate at the other side was too stiff and heavy to open, so everyone leapt over, except Will, who was too short and had to be grabbed and hauled over by the others at the last moment. As they were returning, they passed a slurry ditch which Will suggested they should all jump. The youngest Baber misjudged his leap and fell in. Thoroughly scared, he stood there dripping with black slime and howling, so that finally Will had to get in and drag him out. He knew that they dared not enter the house, so standing at the foot of the steps and using his most wheedling tones he called, "Aunty, will you come here a moment please? Could you come here? I'm sure you could." So that when she eventually appeared, to be confronted by two pairs of eyes staring whitely out of black faces, one scared and one pleading, what could the poor woman do except lift her hands and gasp weakly, "Oh Will, I don't know whether to laugh or cry."

Will was never happier than when he was out in the fields and orchards, either dreaming, wandering on his own, or in the company of others. His companions became aware that he had the need to draw apart from them from time to time, to absorb and to meditate on the beauty of nature and of the countryside and to refresh his spirits, and this need he later expressed in verse:

> O at such times as these
> Only seem I to live!
> Not for the coward peace
> Such hours may give,
> But that my soul may drink
> From some deep hidden stream
> Those flooding ecstasies
> Of more-than-dream.[1]

---

[1] "Solitude", *Ducks and Other Verses*, Sidgwick & Jackson, 1918, p. 30.

But in spite of his tendency to day-dream, Will was full of vitality and energy which he spent in playing games with great zest. Over the years, all but two of the windows at The Redlands were broken by cricket balls. He invented a peculiar game of his own which everyone who came to the house was talked into playing.

Some years later, Leonard Clark was to be one of these victims and he related his experience in his book "A Fool in the Forest".

"You played Harvey's cricket in a long, narrow court, no more than four feet wide, at the back of the house. There were no wickets but only a high wall behind you. The courtyard also had a roof which covered it for half its length. The ball was a hard one, something in size between a cricket and a fives ball. You hit this, or at least tried to hit it, with a shortened hockey stick. You were out if the ball hit the wall three times. Every visitor to that house who had any interest in cricket was pressed to play that version of the game at whatever the season of the year. It had quite a long list of distinguished casualties, including two cathedral organists (bumps on the head), four county batsmen (broken knuckles) and many of the local farmers (normally black eyes). I begin to ache again when I think of my wild efforts at that savage game."[1]

In 1902, when Will was fourteen, it was decided to send him to Rossall School, near Fleetwood in Lancashire. This was at least a year later than most boys go to public school and he entered, not at the beginning of the school year, but in May. Perhaps it was felt that the discipline of a boarding school, together with a complete change of environment, might encourage him to apply himself to his studies.

Certainly the surroundings in which the school was situated could hardly have been a greater contrast to those which surrounded his home. It stands under the sea wall on a very bleak and exposed part of the coastline, often battered by winds off the Irish Sea. The climate is famous for its invigorating properties! At that time the school was quite isolated from the rest of the community, the only transport to Blackpool being a light railway which was out-of-bounds. Only those masters who possessed a trap had freedom of movement.

Soon after he arrived at the school Will had to go through a kind of initiation ceremony called "the fag test" in which all new boys were tested in vocabulary and the traditions of the school and were made to sing the school song or something similar. As a small child he had often been stood on the kitchen table by the farm labourers and taught to sing songs, many of which were vulgar and bawdy and which he

---

[1] Leonard Clark, *A Fool in the Forest*, Dennis Dobson, London 1965, p. 102.

repeated in innocence. This experience, together with his training in memorisation by his governess, stood him in good stead, for among other things he repeated the whole of the Pied Piper.

Later in life Will maintained that it was only his ability at sport which had saved him from being bullied. Games (cricket, hockey, football) were played every afternoon from 2 to 4.

Reminiscing about Rossall School an old boy wrote, "If a boy is fortunate enough to belong to that aristocratic community known as the 'bloods' (i.e. a member of one of the school XI's) he is entitled to wear a special cap provided by the Games Committee, an honour considered by the boys as great as that of winning a University Scholarship."[1] Apparently if a boy was good at games it was a quality which atoned for much.

Will played soccer for the school and the Rossallian brand of hockey on the shore. This was "an adaptation of the Eton Field Game, played with a heavy rubber ball, with light ash sticks, rather like walking sticks. It is a dribbling game with no passing allowed. The basis is a bully or scrum of eight players with two fly halves and a back to support from behind. All 22 players are continually on the move and engaged in the action continually. Although strictly a no-contact game, there is, in fact, a great deal of 'unintentional' physical contact. Not for the frail!"[2] Will won his colours for both hockey and soccer, and once when he was at home, an old aunt remarked, "I like your cap," to which he replied, "The beauty of it is that there are only ten others."

He showed great promise musically and developed a fine tenor or light baritone voice. His mother hoped that he might develop this talent and go on to make a career in music. He gave a number of solo performances in concerts and competitions at the school. *The Rossallian* says of his performance of J.H. Halston's "To Anthea", "His singing was quite a revelation to many of us." In spring 1905, the year he left school, he was awarded the special prize for Broken Voices.

Rossall was a protestant school and as he had already received a sound grounding in the Church of England faith, Divinity was a subject in which he could excel. However, his progress on the academic side was erratic and his position in class varied according to his application to his work, from 4th to 29th, but the school taught independence and this, together with an intractable obstinacy, was a Harvey family trait.

---

[1] *Reminiscences of Rossall School* by J.R.C., an Old Rossallian.
[2] Letter from Mr Peter Bennett, Rossall School.

Will entered the Modern, not the Classical side of the school and at the end of 1902 he received 2nd class honours in Latin, Divinity, English, History and Geography. In 1903 he received 2nd class honours for German. In 1904 he won the German prize for set D and at the end of the same year he gained 1st class honours in Divinity and English and 2nd class honours in German. After this he gained rapid promotion, only to finish 24th in the class.

Although he was 17½ when he left school he never went into the 6th form. In the school records he is listed as going on to be a vet. Possibly he said the first thing that came into his head to satisfy the authorities!

He was glad to leave school, for he had been homesick while there and was a lonely boy. He once told his daughter, "I never learnt a damn thing at Rossall, what I learnt I taught myself." Nevertheless, Rossall, the place, he held in affection in his memory; the sea was a new experience for him and years later he wrote:

> The midnight roar
> Of waves upon the shore
> Of Rossall dear:
> The rhythmic surge and burst
> (The gusty rain
> Flung on the panes!)
> I loved to hear.[1]

In July 1905 Will arrived home with no idea of what he was going to do with his life, and in despair his mother took him to see a phrenologist, who pronounced that he should study law, so arrangements were made for him to be articled to a Mr Treasure in St John's Lane, Gloucester.

---

[1] "The Orchards, the Sea and the Guns", *A Gloucestershire Lad*, Sidgwick & Jackson, 1918, p. 46.

Early Manhood

The years of Harvey's training were happy, carefree ones. He rode into Gloucester daily on horseback, though most unwillingly, and on fine days he played truant, spending hours in the woods and fields, coming home at night as though he had been to the office. He was not paid for his work, so his superiors did not trouble to find out where he had been.

As he revealed in his Self-Portrait, he was an observer of life, and his observations of nature and the countryside were made, not with the eye of a naturalist, but that of a poet. As a boy he had absorbed the beauty that he found around him, and when he became a man, all the impressions that he had stored up came spilling out:

> Sweetness of birdsong shall fall upon my heart,
>   Shall fall upon my heart;
> Nor will I strive to mimic
>   The beauty that I find,
> But lie in a dream and open wide my heart
> And let the song of the birds sink down into my mind.
>
> And the peace that it brings and the joy of joyous things
>   Shall one day brim maybe
>   My heart and brain,
> And I will make a singing of long-forgotten things,
>   And long-forgotten pain,
> Of a heart broken and mended with Beauty in a place
>   Where troubled dreams all ended
>   In birdsong and rain
>   Calling and falling
>   Quietly.[1]

Harvey's upbringing and eduction had fostered in him an interest in the arts, in particular in music and literature and as he grew older his circle of friends included several who were to become well known in their field. Mrs Harvey always welcomed them to The Redlands,

---

[1] "Song", *Ducks and Other Verses*, Sidgwick & Jackson, 1919, p. 66.

where they found an unrivalled hospitality. No-one was ever formally invited to stay for a meal; if they happened to be in the house when a meal was being served, then it was assumed that they would stay to share it. But although there was a flexibility about the number of people who might appear for a meal at any one time, there was certainly no informality about the way in which the meals were presented. If it was tea, then it was served in the drawing-room by a parlour maid who carried in a silver tray and tea-service to grace an already elegantly arranged table. If it was supper, then it was served in the dining room where an abundance of wholesome farm fare, and often a whole Severn salmon, covered the table and sideboard. Mrs Harvey believed in serving her guests in grace and style, but nevertheless everyone was made to feel at home and welcome, and the warmth of the Harveys' hospitality was renowned in the area.

Among the many friends Harvey made during the pre-war years, the closest was Ivor Gurney, the brilliant and erratic Gloucester musician, composer and poet, who became known as The English Schubert. The two had first met and formed a friendship when they were at the King's School. They had so much in common, not only their personal appearance; bespectacled and untidy, but they also shared an intense love of the English countryside.

Gurney almost made The Redlands his second home, for it offered a more educated and artistic background than his own and he had an open invitation to play the grand piano in the drawing-room. In true artist fashion, oblivious of time, he would often arrive during the early hours of the morning, climbing through an unlatched window to begin his passionate playing. Unfortunately, Mrs Harvey's sister, Miss Waters (Aunty Kate) slept in the room above. She was eventually moved to protest and Gurney was requested to reserve his playing for more reasonable hours. He could not understand Miss Waters' lack of appreciation and observed to Harvey, "Oh well, this world is full of Aunty Kates!"

In a scrapbook of his thoughts and ideas, Harvey recorded his pleasure in his friendship with Gurney:

"A memorable evening at home in the music-room after 10 miles walking with Gurney — O joy of dear companionship! Golden curves of Beethoven matching the fire of pear wood burning in the grate with no calm glow of blinking embers but in a golden torment of fantastic flame. Peace was in that hour. Faith binding loveliness. Store of

---

[1] Michael Hurd, *The Ordeal of Ivor Gurney*, Oxford University Press, 1978, p. 23.

courage against life and all it brings. Hinted glory, — glimpses of Heaven.

"On some future day this pencil note shall recall it to me and I shall rise up in strength of remembered beauty to meet all that I thought I could not meet — all that is terrifying to the forgetting mind of a man compassed about with darkness shall become a sighing wind in the night round that stout tower of remembered Beauty."[1]

In later years too, Gurney looked back nostalgically to the happy days he had spent at The Redlands and in his book *Poems* he wrote:

> A creeper-covered house, an orchard near;
> A farmyard with tall ricks upstanding clear
> In golden sunlight of a late September. —
> How little of a whole world to remember!
> How slight a thing to keep a spirit free!
> Within the house were books,
> A piano, dear to me,
> And round the house the rooks
> Haunted each tall elm tree;
> Each sunset crying, calling, clamouring aloud.[2]

Harvey never fully developed his talent for music, though Gurney considered that he had one of the finest drawing-room voices in the country and he had always been an attraction in the parish church for his improvised harmony.

Harvey and Gurney were later joined in their friendship by Herbert Howells, who came from Lydney and was a pupil of Sir Herbert Brewer, the Gloucester organist.

In a radio programme of appreciation after Harvey's death, Howells spoke of his friendship with Harvey and Gurney:

"...Obviously the beginning of it all was the interest all three of us had in music. Harvey was one of the pleasantest amateur singers I ever knew. He had a light baritone voice and had a way of making his singing as interesting as his talk and that is saying a great deal.

"We had extensive walks in which we discussed the universe. I like to recall that in those days, of the three of us, Harvey had by far the greatest common sense. This was before the first world war when things seemed not to have happened to him which made him take quite another turn, both mentally and spiritually. ... He came to live in a world of fantasy and I'd be far from saying that the foundations of that

---

[1] Harvey's Scrapbook, Gloucester County Record Office.
[2] "The Farm", *Poems* by Ivor Gurney. 1919, p. 15.

WALKING SONG

F W HARVEY

IVOR GURNEY

Printed in England

OXFORD UNIVERSITY PRESS, AMEN HOUSE, WARWICK SQUARE, E.C. 4.

A setting of Harvey's poem "Walking Song" by Ivor Gurney.

To
Harry Stevens Davis

SING LULLABY.

Carol-Anthem.

Poem by
F. W. HARVEY.

Music by
HERBERT HOWELLS.

Harvey's poem "Carol" set to music by his friend Herbert Howells.

world had not already been laid ... and of course, he was oblivious of time. That timelessness in Harvey was a comparatively early development. ...

"Harvey ... was a man supersensitive of the sensibilities of other people. You never met a man who didn't like Harvey.

"Harvey and Gurney had two things very much in common. Gurney could meet anyone and talk his language and the gift which Harvey possessed remarkably in those early years was of letting every man blossom in his presence. Every man would reveal himself quite easily to Harvey. ...

"He had a curiously instinctive understanding of the art which was not precisely his. Music was not his art, but I can think of very few people whom I would more willingly talk to about music."[1]

A number of Harvey's poems were set to music by composers such as Howells, Herbert Bedford and Sir Herbert Brewer. The latter composed for his "Gloucestershire Song Cycle" and another cycle of songs called "A Sprig of Shamrock", which was performed at one of the music festivals held in Gloucester. Among Herbert Howells' compositions was a setting of Harvey's "Carol" which is listed in Groves' *Dictionary of Music.*

> Sing lullaby, sing lullaby,
>   While snow doth softly fall,
> Sing lullaby to Jesus
>   Born in an oxen-stall.
>
> Sing lullaby to Jesus,
>   Born now in Bethlehem,
> The naked blackthorn's growing
>   To weave his diadem.
>
> Sing lullaby, sing lullaby,
>   While thickly snow doth fall,
> Sing lullaby to Jesus
>   The Saviour of all.[2]

Musical evenings were a regular feature at The Redlands and no doubt this musical background influenced Harvey's style of writing, for much of it has a lyrical quality.

---

[1] Herbert Howells, "Will Harvey 1888-1957", BBC broadcast produced by Robert Waller, 1958.
[2] "Carol", *Farewell*, Sidgwick & Jackson, 1921, p. 75.

From an early age, Harvey had enjoyed not only the written, but the spoken word. His governess had perhaps sown the first seeds when she had set him to learn poetry and psalms.

Harvey, Gurney and Howells also formed a friendship with J.W. Haines, a local solicitor and literary savant, for whom Harvey was later to work. These four used to meet at The Redlands or J.W. Haines' house, or shared long walks, where they talked music and literature for hours on end, and no doubt, read and discussed Harvey's latest poems.

On 17th August 1913, in a letter to Harvey, Gurney wrote:

"Did I tell you that Haines had seen Abercrombie? who asked Haines whether he knew one named Harvey who showed great promise?"[1]

Apart from this small group of friends, Harvey never showed any interest in belonging to a literary coterie. He belonged to the same generation as The Georgians (in fact he was the same age as Rupert Brooke) and like them he was still writing traditional verse, but he was a provincial and never became a recognised member of the group. In any case, there was soon to be a powerful reaction which was to lead to quite a different style of writing.

Harvey also spent a great deal of his time playing various sports: table tennis, cricket, hockey, football. Brian Frith recalls him throwing himself into the game of table tennis with great zest, dashing from side to side and swearing when he made a bad shot.

Although he had developed such an individualistic style of playing cricket, his technique later took him into the Gloucester City team. Leonard Clark, the poet and author, who had been helped and encouraged by Harvey in his youth, tells how he was at The Redlands one day when Harvey arrived home after playing in a match at Gloucester:

"I later learned from a hypnotised eye-witness that he had scattered the spectators with some terrific off-drives, and almost maimed a fielder for life who had been so foolish as to get in the way of a wicked square cut."[2]

In 1910 he formed a football team among the boys and young men of Minsterworth, headed by himself as their captain, which reformed again after the 1914-18 war. He wrote a special song for them and hundreds of copies of it were sold for 1d each to help raise money for funds for the football club.[3] In spite of his intellect and superior

---

[1] The Gloucester Collection, Gloucester City Library.
[2] Leonard Clark, *A Fool in the Forest*, Dennis Dobson, London 1965, p. 107.
[3] Minsterworth 1850-1957, The Gloucester Collection, Gloucester City Library.

education, he was always happy to be with the village lads, among whom he was very popular.

It was inevitable that Harvey's lack of application to his work would be discovered sooner or later, and at the age of nineteen, when he took his first law examination, not surprisingly, he failed it. His mother took him aside and reproached him, saying, "Will, you *have* to pass this examination, your father has spent a lot of money on you."

This reproach was sufficient to spur him on to make more of an effort to succeed in the work which, in all honesty, bored him, but he loved his mother and hated the thought of failing to live up to her hopes for him. He relied on her practical abilities to keep his life stable and organised. The following year, he took the examination again and passed.

Just before he re-took his examination he received an encouraging letter from Ivor Gurney written in an elated mood, typical of his mental state:

"Buck up Willy my boy, let us have that great elver-fishing scene. You'll have to write short stories first though. In another three weeks I shall be home, and then I'll give you summat to talk about. Priding Point to Bollo Pool, a Sou' wester and a strong ebb-tide and a blue sky, and me taking risks in pure glory of sail and joy of heart and yelling and quoting and singing and hauling at the sheet with my foot brace against the gunwhale, and breaking my arm with holding the tiller.

> Oh that will be
> Glory for me

"I do hope you get through your exam. this time. It is bad enough to go in at all, but to fail it! ... Wow!

> "To try at it again. . . . Woow!
> To . . .
> Nunno! Not so!

"How is your mother — the embodiment of dignity and sweetness to visualise a little. How's Eric and the Motor-bike Merchant and the young Varmer; also the young lidy? [Harvey's brothers and sister]. I wish I were in the bosom of such a family at such a time and place (likewise the aunt).
But ooh Framilode.
One morning I will sail through Bollo Pool up to Minsterworth — an adventure, by Thunder.

Ah well, Willy, these be comforting things to hold in memory and prospect. I hope to share many such with you.

Now, a nice short story...

Neglect not the toilsome sonnet.

Farewell,

Yours

Ivor Gurney."[1]

There is no evidence to show that Harvey ever did try his hand at writing short stories, but the "elver-fishing scene" suggested by Gurney appeared in a humorous poem entitled "Elvers".

> From the Severn river at daybreak come
> Hundreds of happy fishermen home
> With bags full of elvers: perhaps that's why
> We all love Lent,
> Lean mean Lent,
> Fishy old Lent
> When the elvers fry.[2]

Ivor Gurney had gone to London to study at the Royal College of Music, but when he returned to Gloucester in the holidays he and Harvey renewed their walks at all times of the day and night, and enjoyed escapades on the Severn in their shared boat, *The Dorothy*.

> *The Dorothy* was very small: a boat
> Scarce any bigger than the sort one rows
> With oars! We got her for a five-pound note
> At second-hand. Yet when the river flows
> Strong to the sea, and the wind lightly blows,
> Then see her dancing on the tide, and you'll
> Swear she's the prettiest little craft that goes
> Up-stream from Framilode to Bollopool.[3]

Harvey's 21st birthday was celebrated with a picnic on nearby May Hill, one of his favourite spots, whence the whole family, including the servants and labourers, were taken by cart.

Howard Harvey did not live to see his son succeed in qualifying as a solicitor, for his enthusiasm for his horses indirectly led to his

---

[1] Letter from Ivor Gurney to Harvey, The Gurney Archives, Gloucester City Library.
[2] "Elvers", *Farewell*, Sidgwick & Jackson, 1921, p. 29.
[3] "Ballade of River Sailing", *A Gloucestershire Lad*, Sidgwick & Jackson, 1918, p. 9.

premature death at the age of fifty-four. In December 1909 he had been ordered to bed to rest as he had a thrombosis, but it was a market day and he insisted on checking the horses before they set off, groomed and shining, their manes and tails plaited with straw. It was a fine sight which filled him with pride, but it was the last time he was to see it, for he suddenly dropped dead where he stood in the yard.

The day of his funeral the mourning party walked the length of the village, from the house to the church.

Bernard, the youngest son, was being trained to take over the farm as he was the most practical of the children. However, he was later killed in a motorbike accident and so the horses were sold and the land rented out.

Harvey expressed his sadness at the break-up of the farm and the family's association with horses in his poem "The Horses":

> My father bred great horses,
>   Chestnut, grey and brown.
> They grazed about the meadows,
>   And trampled into town.
>
> They left the homely meadows
>   And trampled far away,
> The great shining horses,
>   Chestnut, and brown and grey.
>
> Gone are the horses
>   That my father bred.
> And who knows whither? . . .
>   Or whether starved or fed? . . .
> Gone are the horses,
>   And my father's dead.[1]

In July 1912 Harvey qualified as a solicitor and Gurney, on hearing of his success, wrote to encourage him.

"...Well Will. ... How do you get on? Have you written much? Doesn't this sacred hunger for Spring nourish that fire in you? If it does not yet, get, as I have just got, Davies' Farewell to Poesy, Foliage (his latest book) and Songs of Joy — the finest lyric poetry in English. God Bless the day when Haines recommended that last book to the Gloucester Library. What a Treasury of divine simplicity!

"Willy dear, your photograph is on the piano not far from me as I

---

[1] "The Horses", *Gloucestershire Friends*, Sidgwick & Jackson, 1917, p. 46.

write in bed. Have your confounded family given it their august approval yet? How does the daily round, the common task go? More slippily than formerly I hope. ...

"O Willy, to be well! To stroll around Redlands deep in the keen joy of comparing experience and the taste of verse...

"Don't think your poetic gift will not develop because you have to be at office most of the day. I do not believe it. There are too many examples to the contrary ..."[1]

So Harvey continued to write and was constantly tantalised by those glimpses of divine inspiration which men call Beauty, and attempted to interpret what he saw; he knew that Gurney too was sharing the same experience, as he wrote in one of his letters,

"It's going, Willy. It's going. Gradually the cloud passes, and Beauty is a present thing, not merely an abstraction poets feign to honour."[1]

In a poem dedicated to Beauty, Harvey pledged himself ever to pursue her:

> Yet will I win thee! Never shall men say
> That I have ceased to love and follow thee,
> Tracing thy footsteps howso light they be
> Upon the common dust of every day.[2]

Very early in life Harvey became aware of the importance of Beauty and he once said, "However much money a man may have, if there is no Beauty in his life, he might as well slit his throat." He rejected the kind of life which would lead to a closing of the mind and soul to Beauty's riches, until the soul became blind and sensitivity blunted. He understood the importance of seeing with the soul as well as with the eyes and he knew that this would lead him to the truth beneath the surface of life. It was the immortality of Beauty which inspired the poet, although he was often only vaguely aware of some intangible loveliness, swiftly passing which was gone almost before he was aware of it.

> If Beauty were a mortal thing
> That died like laughter, grief, and lust,
> The poet would not need to sing.[3]

---

[1] Letter from Ivor Gurney to Harvey, The Gurney Archives, Gloucester City Library.
[2] "To Beauty", *Ducks and Other Verses*, Sidgwick & Jackson, 1919, p. 34.
[3] "Triolet", *A Gloucestershire Lad*, Sidgwick & Jackson, 1918, p. 15.

After Harvey qualified, his sheltered, carefree life at home came to an end, and he went to Chesterfield to work as an assistant to a solicitor there. He had to go into digs which was a great hardship after the loving care which he had received from his mother. However, his sense of humour, which was always just below the surface, helped him to make the best of it. He wrote a poem entitled "In Lodgings" in which he described the antics of a mouse in his room while he wrote, and his houseproud landlady slept.

It was during his time at Chesterfield also that he began to consider taking the important step of joining the Roman Catholic Church. It seems that at some time he had had a serious disagreement with a parson on some point and in spite of his previous strong associations with the Church of England, he decided that the Roman Catholic Church would provide him with a set of definite rules by which to abide. He openly admitted, "I entered the Roman Catholic Church because I felt that I needed some discipline in my life and I thought that the Church would provide it."

There was also no doubt something in the ritual and symbolism of the Catholic services which appealed to his sense of beauty, and possibly his argument with the Church of England vicar had been concerned with Puritanism, for he wrote on the subject in his book *Comrades in Captivity*.

"A Puritan is a man who sees things through one window only. But Life has many windows.

> Within this dim five-windowed house of sense
> I watch through coloured glass
> The shapes that pass . . .

"And besides these five windows of the *senses* and the clear glass window of *reason*, there is also *tradition*, a window which looks out upon the past, and the window of *faith* which faces the future.

"Now, since by use of all these windows it is impossible to know God's mysteries, manifestly it is yet more impossible so to do by looking through one window only. But that is just what the Puritan tries to do. . . . This inability to realise more than the brain shows is the chief characteristic of all Puritanism."[1]

All his life Harvey seemed to lack a sense of direction and purpose; he seemed to be searching for an identity. In a scrapbook of jottings which he kept he wrote in 1910:

---

[1] *Comrades in Captivity*, Sidgwick & Jackson, 1920, ch. IV.

"For some time now it has been born on me that I am not yet *Awake*! — that somewhere down beneath this garment of flesh is the *Real Me*, — with the *Real Eyes*. Is it possible that I may one day wake and see things as they are?"[1]

After he left home he must have gone through a period of great disillusionment and despair as the jottings from his scrapbook reveal:

"As for the things I can do people do not think enough of them to give me enough to eat in return. Nor respect me for it but despise me.

> Oh I am helpless
> Hopeless miserable
> God help me

Great sorrows one can bear but to feel like a child little and miserable...
incapable — not understood

> O, it is Hell!
> God save any of us from it!
> It is the only absolute *loneliness*"[1]

And then in 1914 he wrote:

"I am a man looking out for something worth buying — ready to spend all to get it. And I had almost given up hope."[1]

In his poem "Unstable" Harvey showed his recognition of the instability of character which he felt he possessed and throughout his life he was torn between what he wanted to do and what he felt he ought to do, between the person he felt he was and the person he wanted to be.

> A hill in steadfast loveliness
> Wears the morning's misty dress
> Puts on the sunlight's golden crown
> Dons a starry or purple gown;
> But keeps against all weather-fate
> Its own form inviolate;
> And such is the happy destiny
> Of some men. But alas for me,
> I would be steadfast as the hill
> But am as water running still
> The path it must. I would be frozen

---

[1] Harvey's Scrapbook, Gloucester County Record Office.

In ecstacy of some shape chosen —
Whether of joy, whether of pain,
Matters little. I would remain
Finely myself, but consecrate
To beauty be it love or hate.
But when by any known device
Was water fixed unless in ice?
I dimple into good. I eddy
Back into evil, bravely ready
To change again, reflecting ever
My mood: but my desire, never.
O sooner shall the honey bees
Forsake Spring-blossom, than I freeze,
And sooner shall a playing fountain
Turn to rock, than I to mountain.[1]

Harvey took the final steps and was received into the Roman Catholic
Church at Chelmsford, just after he had joined up in the 1st Fifth
Glosters and before being sent to France with many of his
Gloucestershire friends.

---

[1] *Gloucestershire*, Oliver & Boyd, 1947, p. 28.

The War

When Harvey joined the 1st/5th Battalion of the Gloucestershire Regiment in the First World War, he was twenty-six and about to enter a period of his life which was to have a far-reaching effect on him.

He enlisted as a private in 'C' company and those who served with him remembered him as a somewhat unconventional soldier. With his individualistic temperament he did not take kindly to regimentation and in the words of the Company Commander,

"He was a very untidy private, not addicted to spit and polish."[1]

The battalion was trained at Chelmsford where, according to Harvey, it was almost continually raining, and then on the 29th March 1915 they left Folkestone for Boulogne under the command of Lieut. Colonel J.H. Collett. Once in France they were billetted in lofts, barns and even in brewery premises.

Almost as soon as they arrived, the C/E chaplain, Rev. G.F. Helm, launched the *5th Glo'ster Gazette*, the first of the trench newspapers, described by the *Times Literary Supplement* as 'the oldest and most literary of the British Trench Journals.'[2]

Writing in the Introduction to a later, bound edition of the *Gazette*, Rev. Helm said,

"It is no exaggeration to say that the *Gazette*, thanks to the ability of a few contributors, was a success from the very start. In the world of letters, Bishop Frodsham and Mr. E.B. Osborne of the *Morning Post*, to both of whom the *Gazette* owes much, were quick to recognise the genius of Lieut. F.W. Harvey D.C.M., at that time a Lance Corporal in 'C' company. His wealth of imagery, so homely in its hunger for the Malvern Hills, so original in its treatment of the commonplace, marked him out as a poet of no mean order. It was very largely due to his efforts that the *Gazette* survived the very difficult days of its infancy."[3]

In edition No. 4 of the *Gazette*, Rev. Helm wrote, under the heading

---

[1] Col. Waller, B.B.C. programme 'Will Harvey 1888-1957'.
[2] *Times Literary Supplement* October 12th 1916.
[3] *The Fifth Glo'ster Gazette* p. iv.

"Were it not for the untiring and delightful efforts of F.W.H. this paper would have had to discontinue publication."[1]

Harvey quickly became popular with his fellows for his sense of humour and his interest in organising activities to help keep up the men's spirits. He instituted the running of whist drives and the formation of a Debating Society for his platoon. In the report of one of these whist drives in the *Gazette* it states:

"Thirty two players...sat down to the tables, or rather, the waterproof sheets, the ladies being members without hats:...as soon as Lance-Corporal Robertson arrived with a continuous string of prizes...the play became very tense and keen.

"Lance-Corporal Harvey was ever casting a wistful eye on the bottle of champagne, while Private Draper was not unobservant of the pot of jam...

"As the lights failed Lance-Corporal Robertson supplied each set with candles, an action which pleased all until they found at bedtime that it was their own candles which had been burnt.

"Segt. Finch was graciously asked by Sergt. Young to present the prizes, and proceeded to do so with all his well-known esprit and bonhomie. He so praised up the skilful play of Corpls. Harvey and Watkins, expatiated on their generous natures and fondled their prizes so lovingly, that these two winners felt very relieved when at length they did hold the prizes in their own hands.

"Other prizes were likewise handed over with small sermons on the evils of greed, and each winner was called upon for a speech.

"One joke of Corporal Harvey's kept the room rocking for five minutes."[2]

Harvey might have remained in the ranks, had it not been for his ability to get his own way, his power of raising the men's spirits at will, and above all for his unquenchable patriotism.

On 1st August 1915 Harvey received his first promotion, to that of unpaid Lance/Corporal. A few days later he was involved in a night reconnaissance which was to earn him the D.C.M. and a commission. In the words of the citation:

"F.W. Harvey: For conspicuous gallantry on the night of 3rd/4th August, 1915, near Hebuterne, when, with a patrol, he and another Non-commissioned officer went out to reconnoitre in the direction of a suspected listening post. In advancing they encountered the hostile

---

[1] *The Fifth Glo'ster Gazette* Page 17.
[2] *The Fifth Glo'ster Gazette* No. 5 August 1915.

post evidently covering a working party in the rear. Corporal Knight at once shot one of the enemy and, with Lance-Corporal Harvey, rushed the post, shooting two others and, assistance arriving, the enemy fled. Lance Corporal Harvey pursued, felling one of the retreating Germans with a bludgeon. He seized him, but finding his revolver empty and the enemy having opened fire, he was called back by Corporal Knight, and the prisoner escaped. Three Germans were killed and their rifles and a Mauser pistol were brought in. The patrol had no loss."

The bludgeon referred to was a threshing flail belonging to a French farmer which Harvey had no doubt found lying in the fields. He kept the stick as a souvenir and referred to it as "My medal winner."

When Harvey was decorated in the field, the men must have been struck by his smallness of stature for the remark went round, "They'll say (the Germans), 'If the little buggers be like that, what'll the big 'uns be like?'."[1] Indeed, his unprepossessing appearance made it difficult to believe that he was capable of an heroic act, and this was remarked upon in a letter, written by someone who had met him shortly afterwards.

"I met Harvey when I was going home on promotion. Someone pointed him out to me as a D.C.M. I never saw anyone less like a hero in my life. Imagine a small, dirty, nearly middle-aged man* wearing glasses and an apologetic air, trudging alone the pavé under a huge pack (he looked more like a learned tortoise than anything else I can think of) grasping a huge, hardwood bludgeon — the bludgeon he did the deed with. I remember saying to a Gloucestershire private, 'Your D.C.M. looks as if he stuffed birds in civilian life,' and we called him 'the bird stuffer' all the way to Blighty.

"He was, I think, taking the bludgeon home to his mother, and was most apologetic about his medal when I congratulated him."[2]

After their decoration, Harvey and Knight returned to England for a course of officer training on Hayling Island. While there they were able to return to Gloucester to receive personal congratulations from the City Council. Harvey was also congratulated by an alderman representing the solicitors of the city, and in thanking them Harvey remarked that he had heard it said that a solicitor *should* make a good soldier because he always knew how to charge!

Once they had been commissioned, Harvey and Knight returned to the battlefield, this time in the 2nd battalion. Sadly, Second Lieut.

[1] *The Forest of Dean*, Brian Waters 1951 Chapter 15.
[2] *Comrades in Captivity* F.W. Harvey, Sidgwick & Jackson 1920 Chap. V.
* In fact he was twenty-seven.

An untypically tidy Will Harvey on passing his final law exam in 1912.
By courtesy of Mr Melville Watts

Mr and Mrs Howard Harvey, with Will and brother Eric.
By courtesy of Mr Melville Watts

Left: In the Great War, F.W. Harvey won the D.C.M. for 'conspicuous gallantry'.
Right: F.W. Harvey c. 1950.   *By courtesy of Mr Patrick Harvey*

The Redlands, Minsterworth. Will Harvey's childhood home.
By courtesy of Mrs S. Venables

An open book on the Harvey family pew in St. Peter's Church, Minsterworth.
By courtesy of Mrs S. Venables

Top: Rossall School, Fleetwood as Harvey would have known it.
By courtesy of Mr Peter Bennett

Bottom: The converted railway carriages on the banks of the Severn at Broadoak where Harvey lived while working at Newnham.

Knight died of wounds on 25th July 1916 and Harvey wrote this Memoriam:

> Dear, rash, warm-hearted friend,
> So careless of the end,
> So worldly-foolish, so divinely-wise,
> Who, caring not one jot
> For place, gave all you'd got
> To help your lesser fellow-men to rise.
>
> Swift-footed, fleeter yet
> Of heart. Swift to forget
> The petty spite that life or men could show you:
> Your last long race is won,
> But beyond the sound of gun
> You laugh and help men onward — if I know you.[1]

After his return to France, Harvey became quite a joke in the trenches for the way in which he would walk around carrying a large revolver and laying odds on whether he would come out of the trenches alive or whether he would be wounded, but the idea of being taken prisoner seemed never to have entered his head.

On one occasion Harvey and his sergeant had been given orders to go out into No Man's Land, in the middle of which there was a large crater, to discover the position of a sniper who had been firing at their trenches and killing a number of men.

They set off, Harvey with his large revolver and his sergeant carrying several small grenades. There was a derelict house in the middle and when they reached it the two men sat down quietly on a pile of bricks wondering what to do next. Suddenly, down below them, a man coughed. They were so startled that Harvey pulled his revolver trigger, missing the sergeant by a fraction. This was the only time the sergeant had seen Harvey use his revolver.

Ivor Gurney knew Harvey well enough to understand what an effect the experiences of war might have on his friend. As he wrote to his mentor, Miss Marion Scott, in October 1915:

"... There is little to tell you about F.W. Harvey. He is, perhaps was, my best friend, and a man almost without blot. He has never had good health and so has not yet been able to prove himself; war does not suit weak nerves either. Let's hope he'll get what our gallant soldiers

---

[1] "To R.E.K. (In Memoriam)", *Gloucestershire Friends*, Sidgwick & Jackson, 1917, p. 39.

call a 'blight', a wound bad enough to incapacitate, but good enough to come home with..."[1]

But in August 1916, a year after he had won the D.C.M., Harvey was taken prisoner. It was typical of him that he was captured alone. In fact, his disappearance caused a good deal of trouble to those left behind in his trench.

When he was first missed, his sergeant was sent along to his dugout to look for him. His tunic was still hanging there and by the side of the remains of a bottle of whisky he had left a note, "Gone over to catch a German." For several days periscopes were used to look for him and for three nights running his sergeant was sent out to search for him, expecting to find him dead in No Man's Land. He was finally reported "Missing, believed killed". Eventually, of course, the news of his capture filtered through and in time his name appeared on two plaques in the village church, one showing all those who enlisted and the other, those wounded or taken prisoner.

In his book, *Comrades in Captivity*, which he wrote soon after the war, he recorded, "The circumstances of my capture were, to say the least of them, unusual. To put it baldly, I was taken alone in a German front-line trench, which I had entered unseen yet in broad daylight and was proceeding to explore. It sounds incredibly rash and silly. Perhaps it is neither so incredibly rash nor so silly as it sounds. Certainly it was up to a point the prettiest bit of patrolling I ever did. Certainly it was the identical rashness which got me a decoration in 1915 that got me taken prisoner in 1916."[2]

He went on to describe how, as a platoon commander, he was entrusted with company patrolling, admitting that his methods were generally considered to be unconventional. It was his practice to make a personal examination of the ground to be patrolled before taking his men over it. On this occasion he set off while all was quiet during the rest hour, using the shadow of a hedge which terminated in front of the enemy parapet. But having achieved his object, his sense of adventure was not satisfied, and being alone and all being quiet in the enemy trench, he decided to enter it, though not without a little conscience-searching before doing so.

"Reason told me at this point that it would be better to go back. What a little thing in human life is reason! Besides, there were at least three reasons against doing so. These were, first, and of course chiefly, that I did not want to go back, having come so far, without some

---

[1] The Gurney Archives, Gloucester City Library.
[2] *Comrades in Captivity*, Introductory Chapter, Sidgwick & Jackson, 1920.

evidence (e.g. cap or rifle) to corroborate my report and to show the men who were new to patrol work how easy it was...

"It would be quite possible, so I had told my colonel the day before, for a scout to lie up there [in the long grass above the trench] the whole night, taking note of the position of the trench mortars and machine-gun emplacements, and I had offered to prove it to him. 'Umph!' he had said with a smile, 'we shall see.' This I took as sanction to the attempt which I had certainly not designed to achieve when I set out on that particular afternoon, but which, so it seemed, was likely to be accomplished by mere force of circumstances if my luck held good."[1]

But his luck did not hold good. He heard footsteps behind him and scurrying through the trench, was unable to find holes through the parados such as the British trenches possessed. He was seized by two large Germans, one of whom, as he said, 'looked so ridiculously like a certain labourer on my father's farm in England that I simply burst out laughing, which possibly saved my life.'[1]

In spite of the tremendous risk which he had taken in entering an enemy trench, Harvey's first reaction on being taken prisoner was one of disbelief. He seemed to have regarded his activities as a soldier in the same way that he had the escapades of his youth and he had apparently never even considered the possibility of being taken captive.

The news of his disappearance was a great shock to his family and friends. In a letter to Miss Marion Scott, Ivor Gurney wrote:

"The thing that fills my mind most though is, that Willy Harvey, my best friend, went out on patrol a week ago, and never came back. It does not make very much difference: for two years I have had only the most fleeting glimpses of him, but we were firm enough in friendship, and I do not look ever for a closer bond, though I live long and am as lucky in friendship as heretofore. He was full of unsatisfied longings. A Doctor would have called it neurasthenia, but that term covers many things, and in him it meant partly an idealism that could not be contented with realities. His ordinary look was gloomy, but on being spoken to, he gladdened one with the most beautiful of smiles, the most considerate courtesy of manner. Being self-absorbed, he was nevertheless nobly unselfish at most times, and all who knew him and understood him must not only have liked him merely but loved him. Had he lived, a great poet might have developed from him, could he only obtain the gift of serenity.

"As a soldier, or rather as I would say, a man, he was dauntlessly brave and bravery in others stirred him not only to the most generous recog-

---

[1] *Comrades in Captivity*, Introductory Chapter, Sidgwick and Jackson 1920.

nition, but also unfortunately to an insatiable desire to surpass that. His desire for nobility and sacrifice was insatiable and was at last his doom, but his friends may be excused for desiring a better ending than that probable, of a sniper's bullet in No Man's Land. There is only one thing to make me glad in all this, which is — that I saw him a few hours before he went out, and he lent me his pocket edition of Robert Bridges' 'Spirit of Man', a curious collection, but one well worth having; and a worthy memory of my friend. I need no such remembrances; if the Fates send that I live to a great age and attain fulness of days and honour, nothing can alter my memory of him or the evenings we spent together at Minsterworth. My thoughts of Bach and all firelit frosty evenings will be full of him, and the perfectest evening of Autumn will but recall him the more vividly to my memory. He is my friend, and nothing can alter that; and if I have the good fortune ever to meet with such another, he has a golden memory to contend with."[1]

After he was taken prisoner, Harvey was kept in solitary confinement for ten days in a small, dirty, louse-ridden room in Douai. During this time he began to realise what captivity was going to mean. He discovered an old French book lying in the room and on the flyleaf he wrote a poem entitled 'Solitary Confinement' in which he said that in spite of his apparent solitude, he had the company of the sun, the wind and the moon, all of which stirred up memories to provide him with companions.

At the end of ten days he was moved to a disused lunatic asylum at Gütersloh, the first of seven prison camps he was to experience in his two years of captivity.

The Introduction to Harvey's last book of poems, *Gloucestershire* published in 1947 was written by a fellow P.O.W. who said:

"In 1916, into the P.O.W. camp of Gütersloh, Westphalia, there came a thick-set, swarthy little man of the 5th Glosters, who had been captured on individual patrol inside the German trenches. This was F.W. Harvey. In his own regiment he had the reputation of a man who expected to be left in peace to write poetry except when there was dangerous work on hand, and had won the D.C.M. for prowess in No Man's Land. In captivity where each man must make his contribution to the common life, we were soon proud of him too. In a camp of a thousand Russians, French, Belgians and British of all our nations and colonies he was our only poet, he was our best singer of songs, he

---

[1] Letter from Ivor Gurney to Miss Marion Scott, 24th August 1916, from The Gurney Archives, Gloucester City Library.

played games well and was always ready for a dash for freedom on his own. I saw him carried out of the camp in an ominously creaking wicker basket, I helped to screen him from the guards when he jumped from a fast moving train... One of the qualities that drew men of so many countries and nationalities to Harvey was the intensity of his local patriotism, his deep feeling for his home. To the core he is Gloucestershire, the poet of its people, its farms, its churches, its pubs, the Severn, Cotswolds, The Forest of Dean, and to this Scots and Irish, Colonials and Allies warmed as to a voice from their own home."

Thus began a time of Harvey's life which, paradoxically, was to stimulate and inspire him more than any other. He was able to study his fellows at close quarters; their camaraderie and loyalty, their determination to keep up their morale, their attempts at escape, and above all, their respect and affection for him, gave him a purpose in life which perhaps before had been lacking.

In January 1921, in reply to a request for details about himself from someone he wrote "...war broke out in 1914. The 8th August in that year saw him wearing a private's uniform in the 5th Glos: Regt/and for the first time in his life he became really useful since he was able, as a prisoner's friend, to appear in two courts martial of men accused of sleeping on guard and (by dint of a ruthless cross examination of his superior officers) obtain their aquital." (sic)[1]

The days in the camp, tedious though they were in some respects, had a framework and pattern which he needed. As he said himself,

"I know that never again in this life shall I hold so high and happy a position among my fellows."[2]

Every prisoner was expected to contribute something of value to the life of the camp and as Harvey could write, sing and play games he was soon much in demand. He lectured, wrote poems and essays, and 'The Poet' became his camp title. It was soon discovered that his unprepossessing appearance belied his capabilities. On one occasion, when he was spoken of disparagingly by a senior officer to another yet more senior, the latter was heard to remark,

"Just wait until you hear him speak."

As a prisoner, Harvey continued to fight, yet not in bloody battle against a tangible foe, but against self-pity, cowardice, selfishness and what he called the 'green mould of the mind.' He would not allow his mind to be overcome by external conditions, but created within himself another world, which, although a way of escape, he did not

---

[1] Harvey's Scrapbook, Gloucester County Record Office.
[2] *Comrades in Captivity*, Chapter 11, Sidgwick & Jackson, 1920.

consider to be escapism but flight to the freedom of the mind. At times
he almost slipped into desperate moods, when his spirit was very near
to darkness and life appeared to be nothing more than re-living the
past, when he felt that he and his fellow-prisoners were in danger of
stagnating:-

> Laugh, Oh laugh loud all ye who long ago
> Adventure found in gallant company!
> Safe in Stagnation, laugh, laugh bitterly,
> While on this filthiest backwater of Time's flow
> Drift we and rot, till something set us free!
>
> Laugh like old men with senses atrophied,
> Heeding no Present, to the Future dead,
> Nodding quite foolish by the warm fireside
> And seeing no flame, but only in the red
> And flickering embers, pictures of the past: –
> Life like a cinder fading black at last.[1]

The freedom of the spirit during captivity was of great importance to
Harvey, and his striving to free his own and that of his fellows is clearly
shown in his book *Comrades in Captivity*.

The servants of his 'other life' were imagination and memory. He
was able to call up memories of the past at will and these sustained him:

> Now joy is dead and hope o'er cast
> I call a dream out of the past
> And thus command him: "Slave, go bring
> Out of my days one day in spring
> And out of *that* a certain hour
> Which glimmers through an April shower,
>   Let apple-blossom crown the day,
>   And heap the hedges white with may!"
>
> 'Tis done. In one great backward surge
> Of time the Past and Present merge:
> For Time is not a drifting river,
>   A moment here, then past forever;
> And what is done in the heart's deep core
>   Is done not once but for evermore.[2]

One can understand how painful prison life in a strange country

---

[1] "Prisoners", *Gloucestershire Friends*, Sidgwick & Jackson, 1917 p. 17.
[2] "A Memory", *Ducks and other Verses*, Sidgwick & Jackson, 1919, p. 63.

must have been to a man so much a part of his own country. Its beauty and its character had been so absorbed into his life that to be apart from it was almost to lose part of himself. His desire to hold home in his heart and mind filled him with an uneasy dread and suspicion. He could not bear to think that all that for which he and others had been fighting might be changed on their return and he hoped that men would value their country even more highly, knowing what a great price had been paid to save it.

If we return, will England be
Just England still to you and me?
The place where we must earn our bread?
We, who have walked among the dead,
And watched the smile of agony,

And seen the price of Liberty,
Which we have taken carelessly
From other hands. Nay, we shall dread
If we return.[1]

Harvey believed war to be the call of Honour and Duty and his great desire was to fashion a new England; that men should fight, not only for love of their country, but in the belief that, if victory were obtained, the understanding that had grown up between all classes in battle and captivity should continue in peace and freedom. He did not desire war, yet he felt that his country fought for that which was right. For him, committing an act of patriotism in wartime meant that one might hate the act itself, yet one did it with all one's might, using the deed as an offering of self-sacrifice to God, giving oneself completely for one's brothers in order to further the cause for which one was fighting.

Four years after the war, the question of patriotism was still very much on his mind and he wrote an article on the subject for his local paper:

"...A rationalist cannot be a patriot. He may fight for his country. He can no more be a patriot than he can understand the Holy Sacrament. For patriotism is not merely to fight, to die for one's country. It is not even to live for her. It is to see her, and to see her glorified, when at the solemn moment bread and wine are no longer upon the altar, but God!...Patriotism has in essence nothing to do

---

[1] "If we Return", *A Gloucestershire Lad*, Sidgwick & Jackson, 1918, p. 25.

with possession — with having and holding. It is nothing taken. It has only to do with something given — the patriot; and given again to him in return — what? A promise and a vision..."[1]

War can have a sickening effect upon the mind. At those times when England appeared very distant, the knowledge that only those who were fighting truly understood the meaning of war, engendered bitterness and cynicism, when the noise and heat of battle rose and bodies fell around them, the soldiers imagined those at home carrying on their normal, everyday life:

> We have taken a trench
>   Near Combles, I see,
> Along with the French
> We have taken a trench.
> (*Oh, the bodies, the stench!*)
> Won't you have some more tea?
>   We have taken a trench
> Near Combles, I see.[2]

The sight of death and the effect of war upon the living probably sickens the mind more than actual participation in the fight, when there is no time to stop and reflect and the mind becomes detached. But as soon as there is a lull and a pause in physical activity, the reality of the situation floods in, bringing either complete revulsion, or a closing of the mind which plants the feet firmly on the path to cynicism:

> But O you piteous corpses yellow-black,
>   Rotting unburied in the sunbeam's light,
> With teeth laid bare by yellow lips curled back
>   Most hideously; whose tortured souls took flight
>   Leaving your limbs, all mangled by the fight,
> In attitudes of horror fouler far
>   Than dreams which haunt the devil's brain at night;
> Because of you I loathe the name of War.[3]

Yet the thought of death and life beyond it held no fear for the poet; although it was a mystery, it was not an enemy. His life was valuable to him, and for the moment sufficient, with all its strangeness and beauty,

---

[1] 'Patriotism', The Gloucester Journal, 22.4.22
[2] 'At Afternoon Tea', *Gloucestershire Friends*, Sidgwick & Jackson 1917, page 44.
[3] 'Ballade No 1', *Gloucestershire Friends*, Sidgwick & Jackson, 1917, page 27.

but one cannot doubt his readiness for death had it come upon him, even should he have been forced to inflict it on himself, as he wrote in *Comrades in Captivity*:

"...it had always been my rule, since I did much patrol work, to carry in my pocket sufficient morphia to finish myself off in the event of my being left out in No Man's Land, a dying torment to myself and a living danger to such as might be tempted to drag me in."

He was ready to give his life and to meet death, and the reason he gave for his being spared was that his willingness did not show the right qualities of sacrifice:

> My undevout yet ardent sacrifice
> Did God refuse, knowing how carelessly
> And with what curious sensuality
> The coloured flames did flicker and arise.
> Half boy, half decadent, always my eyes
> Sparkle to danger: Oh it was joy to me
> To sit with Death gambling desperately
> The borrowed Coin of Life . . .[1]

These few lines reveal so much about the poet's character and temperament. In his war poems he tried to express what he had learnt from his experiences. Naturally they were affected by his moods of patriotic fervour, grief and occasional bitterness, but through them all rose that great human and divine quality of love. The love which embraced his country, his home, his fellow men. Harvey's attitude to life and death was summed up in a letter which he wrote to his mother from the trenches:

"...Those who have not been in the trenches think it should create a sympathetic yearning over life and the so-transitory gleam. In peace-time they could write of the 'little emptiness of love', (you see, Rupert Brooke was not guiltless!) but that was in peace-time. Here we do not mourn the shortness of life because of love, nor, (more cynically) the shortness of love out-lived by living. The fellowship of death has taught us better and truer things. Yet, because death is strange, pray humanly that the cup may pass from me, dear mother. Pray that (as is permissible), but never grieve if it is not so, for God's ways are glorious and past finding out in his *love* for the children of men."[2]

While a prisoner, Harvey was less concerned with the futility and bloodiness of war than were some other poets, such as Wilfred Owen

---

[1] 'Sonnet', *Gloucestershire Friends*, Sidgwick & Jackson, 1917, page 18.
[2] Letter to his mother from F.W. Harvey, *Fifth Glo'ster Gazette*.

and Siegfried Sassoon. In the preface to his book of poems, *A Gloucestershire Lad at home and abroad* it was noted that "Mud, blood and khaki are rather conspicuously absent from Mr. Harvey's poems." The futility which *he* felt was his own inability to share the battle with those still fighting, and his desire, like that of his fellow prisoners, was to escape.

However, he did not join in the escape plans of the others; he remained an individualist even in this. He was not interested in the long-drawn-out discipline of tunnelling. His first plan was to jump out of one of the windows at Schwarstadt prison, onto a telegraph pole, sliding the twenty feet or so to the ground. Fortunately, on the day that he was going to make the attempt, someone noticed that barbed wire had been twined up the pole for several feet, so he had to wait for another opportunity.

Some time later someone in the camp offered him a suit of civilian clothes, and these he put by until he and some others were being transferred to another camp by train. While his companions distracted the attention of the sentry, he got into the clothes and jumped out of the train. Although his landing was painful he was not seriously hurt, but his flight was noticed by a group of people in the fields reaping. He blamed his recapture on the German characteristic of correctness in all things. To jump from a train was 'verboten' so they gave chase, caught him and took him to the police, who accused him of being a spy and of planning to blow up the railway tunnel. In order to save himself from the punishment of death for spying, he had to confess that he was a British officer and so had to endure the lesser punishment of solitary confinement.

Although he did not join in the tunnelling and other joint escape projects, he did draw upon his legal training to help his brother officers. This was completely unofficial and secret, though the Germans may have suspected what was going on. In his book *Comrades in Captivity* he described it thus:

". . . the best line of defence" [in a court martial] "to whatever questions had to be answered, was thought out, written down and learnt by heart...it was then translated into German. At trial the translated defence was handed to the judges. The prisoner did not require a German counsel. He had written out his defence...The court was naturally pleased at this saving of time..."[1]

On another occasion his legal training helped him to extricate himself from a difficult situation. It was discovered that someone had

---

[1] Chapter XXIV, *Comrades in Captivity*, Sidgwick & Jackson, 1920.

been trying to cut the camp wire and a search revealed a number of escape kits which naturally no-one claimed. As a punishment, the Commandant ordered all the officers in the three suspected rooms to report every hour at the interpreter's office. The officers all agreed not to go, as the British and German governments had agreed to ban collective punishments.

The next day the men were sent for and questioned in turn. As Harvey was at the end of the line, he had time to think and realised that the Commandant was trying to obtain a signed admission of guilt which Harvey determined not to give. When his turn came, he argued so skilfully that he succeeded in having the Commandant's order cancelled.

The news that he had not been killed but was a prisoner and had endured several spells of solitary confinement filtered through to his friends and Ivor Gurney wrote to encourage him.

"My dear Old Willy,

It's a dull day. I will comfort and Renew myself by writing to you, friend of orchard and river; drawing life from memories of blue and silver seen together and sights of sunset from the little hill . . .How are you now, being out of solitary confinement and able to mix with men again? You must be happier surely. Are your parcels coming? Your mother said you had not been getting them regularly when she last heard.

"Dear chap, there's so much to talk about. I'll put my hand on your shoulder, and we'll wander about the fields and roads to talk of the Georgian Book No. 3 — which has several new names. (Willy, I hope you'll be in No. 4).

"These young writers are very interesting, very much in earnest and very gifted; out of him a great poet should come.

"Make haste Willy and start it!
O we'll do such things together yet!
You must be stale with imprisonment; but still, unless weak with hunger and sickness — force yourself: write . . .

"O you just wait! Once you are back I'll fill you to the neck with music and wonderfully subtle criticisms of your own and other poetry . . .

. . ."I think I shall be able to help you quite a lot old boy, and strongly hope so . . .
I have been playing the piano — not a bad one — in the Reception Room here, and there is no doubt Willy that I play better than ever in my life. I longed for you to hear some of the stuff I went through — a most appreciative audience you were always, and when you come back (If circumstances permit) I'll set you writing in no time . . .

"Do you remember how in Spring evenings, the gold of late sunlight

41

used to be heavy on the floor of the orchard that lies to the right of the road nearing your house on a journey from Gloucester? and great sunsets? and Autumn afterglow most tender, most 'thronged'? (You know what I mean). You'll make words to catch that charm, and I'll make music, combine the result.

Cherrio Willy, things will come right in the end. Look at me — the sick creature of 4 years ago, and what I am now. If *I* can do it, what can you do?

"Though you have to live on the last ultimate scrap of grit in your being — some day you'll live easily in Joy, because you like living for its sweet and varied interests, and think of any evil of the past as a necessary light price for so much content. Dear old Willy, if friendship is anything at all, you should be happy, for there cannot be one friend of all your many forgets or has forgotten you, who have the power of holding from a distance as only Great Lovers can — of increasing it, indeed."[1]

Gurney had a book of his own poetry published in which several poems were dedicated to F.W.H. One, "Afterglow", being a nostalgic reference to the autumn afterglow mentioned in his letter.

Harvey himself was trying to promote an interest in Gurney's work and wrote to him from Crefeld in 1917:

"My dear Old Chap,

"I am delighted to hear of the London Orchestral Concert and your growing fame.

"By the way: Do you want to make a lot of money? If so, publish 'The Old Bold Mate' either in a set of drinking songs or by itself. *And stick out for a royalty.*

"I have sung it in three battalions and in two prisoners' camps and *everywhere* it has been a great success.

"Here it is a household thing and I have had to write out dozens of copies. By this means it will be known all over Scotland, Wales, Ireland, Canada, Argentina etc., within a few years of peace and you ought to reap what grain is forthcoming.

"Your best things will not pay you very well I expect, but this jolly piece of fooling should make your fortune.

"I am serious — and have nothing else to tell you.

Always yours affectionately,

F.W.H."[2]

---

[1] Letter from Ivor Gurney to F.W. Harvey, The Gloucester Collection, Gloucester City Library.

[2] Letter from F.W.H. to Ivor Gurney, The Gloucester Collection, Gloucester City Library.

It was while he was a prisoner that Harvey heard the song 'Waltzing Matilda' and first introduced it in England when he published his book *Comrades in Captivity*. Later a Dr. Thomas Wood wrote down the words and music and it quickly became popular.

Throughout the time that he was in captivity Harvey continued to write and his poems were sent home, eventually being published in two small volumes.

The first book, *A Gloucestershire Lad at Home and Abroad*, came out in September 1916 and was dedicated to 'All comrades of mine who lie dead in foreign fields for love of England or who live to prosecute the war for another England.' It contained a preface by his commanding officer, Colonel Collett and was reviewed in the trench newspaper *The Fifth Glo'ster Gazette* by Bishop Frodsham, a canon residentiary at Gloucester cathedral who said, "The secret of Mr Harvey's power, is that he says what other English lads 'in Flanders' want to say and cannot." He concluded his review by saying,

"Sufficient has been said to show that this modest little volume has real charm, and not a little depth of thought and beauty. It contains far more real poetry than many a volume ten times its length, ushered into the world with sycophantic fanfaronade."[1]

Ivor Gurney had been delighted to hear that Harvey was safe, even if a prisoner and rejoiced in the news in a letter to Miss Scott in 1916:

"Yes the news about Harvey is very tray bong. He is probably safer there (at this stage of the war) than anywhere; and so 'everything in the garden's lovely' as the music-hall song saith. It is a wonderful piece of luck though. His brother has gained the Military Cross at the Somme, his other brother is in one of the tanks; a remarkable family, with a sister quite ready to do the same...

"F.W.H.'s book did not contain much of his best work. It was meant to get him in the public eye while it was still open to such things. There is some perfect work, some good, some pretty good, some slipshod and some downright bad. But 'Flanders' is a star..."[2]

Gurney was so impressed by this poem that he set it to music and sent it to his old friend Herbert Howells at the Royal College of Music. In a letter to Miss Scott, Howells wrote:

"...I feel I must tell you that this afternoon I again brought forward Gurney's two songs — 'In Flanders' and 'By a Bierside' — at a lesson with Sir Charles. I played them to him (and to Dr. Wood) and both were most enormously impressed by their beauty. Sir C. forgot his

[1] *The Gloucester Gazette* December 1916.
[2] The Gurney Archives, The Gloucester Collection, Gloucester City Library.

week-old criticisms — except for one or two details — and at once said they *must* be done at the second orchestral concert this term. I am going to attempt the scoring of them...
I hope the news of this will hearten the dear warrior . . ."[1]

However, *A Gloucestershire Lad* had a critical reception in the *Times Literary Supplement*, as Gurney remarked in a letter to Marion Scott:
"...Did you see the review of F.W.H's book in the T.L.S.? Golly, but there is nothing to give my poor friend a swelled head in that notice!"[1]

Harvey admitted that much of the poetry which he wrote, especially while in solitary confinement, was poor, often written simply to exercise his brain, and it was unfortunate that it appears to have been collected together indiscriminately, rather than the best being selected for publication in one rather than two volumes.

Gloucestershire Friends was dedicated to 'The best of all Gloucestershire Friends, my Mother'. This was a collection of poems sent home to his mother from the camps, again uncensored by the German authorities. The keynote of this poetry was nostalgia, for he was stirred by a great longing for his home county. In October 1916 a long article appeared in the *Times Literary Supplement* on Trench Literature, in which the writer said:
"There is an element of what the Russians call prostor (the opening of the heart to vastness) in the British soul, which cannot find full contentment in the garden labyrinths and poplar-sentinelled highways of the French countryside, but longs for the wide prospects and spacious parks and mist-veiled heights of his native island."[2]

This was particularly true of Harvey. Even in sleep the longing did not leave him and wound itself about his dreams until they became almost a reality:

> At night, in dream,
> I saw those fields round home
> > Agleam.
> Drenched all with dew
> Beneath day's newest dome
> > Of gold and blue.

---

[1] The Gloucester Collection, Gloucester City Library.
[2] The *Times Literary Supplement*, October 12th 1916.

All night —
All night they shone for me, and then
    Came light.
And suddenly I woke, and lovely joy!
I was at home, with the fields gold as when
    I was a boy.[1]

The review of *Gloucestershire Friends* in the *Morning Post* said:

"He has used the weary days of captivity to good purpose, for his new poems show an advance in technique, and also a fuller and deeper sense of the function of poetry as a 'criticism of life' ... every piece in his new volume shows that the English heart is unconquerable in adversity ...

"Here is a little book of the munitions of memory and hope, which will be a proof to after-ages that even a German prison camp could not tarnish the bright valiancy of English soldiers."[2]

Another review in the trench paper said ... "this book is even better than the first. The poems are of the same stamp as before, all short and all sincere. The conventions of war poetry are, as before, flouted. The poems are the true expressions of real emotion ... In sincerity of feeling and in purity of melody Mr. Harvey is worthy to stand with the Caroline Lyrists."[3]

The *Glasgow Herald* wrote: "This is a book with great beauty in it and great courage — a reader indeed feels very small face to face with the sunlit and lovelit resolution that gives it its power."

It was the *Cheltenham Chronicle* which gave him the title of Laureate of Gloucestershire in its review, which said, "We place Rupert Brooke first among the many soldier-poets produced by this war. But in purely lyric, singing quality, none has done better than Lieut. F.W. Harvey, who may be described not inaptly as The Laureate of Gloucestershire."

The *Welsh Outlook* was particularly impressed by the poem "The Bugler" which it quoted in full and said, "The book contains some poems equal to anything Mr. Harvey has written, and one certainly superior. Verse such as this would compensate for a deal of light metal, and a poet who can write it should have many volumes of the real stuff of poetry before him."

In letters to Marion Scott, Gurney wrote a number of comments on

---

[1] The Awakening, *A Gloucestershire Lad*, Sidgwick & Jackson, 1918, p. 27.
[2] *The Morning Post*, 3rd October 1917.
[3] *The Gloucester Gazette*, November 1917.

the two books, apparently in answer to some criticisms by her.

"...The writer is obviously at the beginning of his strength and has not yet gained mastery. Some pieces have been written under pressure of time and lack form chiefly on that account.

"...As to the attitudes taken by certain writers to the present time and to their land; don't forget that this usually represents what they wish to think and on some rare occasions do. These are intense moments and live in memory afterwards when the exercise of writing is sometimes used to recreate an emotion."

"...My poor friend was tired: do not judge him by this. It is the ineffectual beating of wings, a sick mind's desire. So fine a footballer, cricketer, man, cannot wait many years after the war for his fulfilment. *This* is not it, anyway. It will do as a source of quotation for Bishop Frodsham, who will also obtain a pleasurable glow of satisfaction at his great work of uplifting the people by Literature.

"Will Harvey is an untidy, careless dreamer who has known much sorrow, chiefly because his mind was not occupied as fully as it needed to be. He is chivalry itself, and the detection of Fear within his heart is merely the spur to action. He sings well — and is indeed born a lover of all Beauty. He is capable of great Wisdom, of glorious foolishness. Loves Life which loves not him. Some men have to form themselves, to control their every tiniest movement of spirit, and indeed to create their own world. And such is he, who has now learnt all bitter things, and has only to gather the sweet with experienced hand. A mind of sweetness allied to strength which has never known itself and cannot live as most men by habit. But don't look at *Gloucestershire Friends* to find all this."[1]

Strangely enough Gurney does not mention Harvey's sense of humour, which, in addition to his religious faith, helped to sustain him during his imprisonment. On one occasion, when he had just been released from one of his spells of solitary confinement, he found that one of his room-mates had drawn over his bed a picture of a pool of water, on which floated some white ducks, and this inspired him to write his best-known poem, "Ducks". It now appears in many anthologies, and during the last war, one of the English exercises in German schools was to translate "Ducks" into German. When he was told this Harvey said, "Serves the Germans damn well right!" and it certainly cannot have been an easy exercise:

---

[1] Letter from Ivor Gurney to Miss Marion Scott, October 8th 1917, from the Gurney Archive, Gloucester City Library.

Ducks

BY

Frederick Wm Harvey

This poem was written at night in Holzminden Prison, inspired by a drawing on the wall of the prison dormitory where Harvey was a P.O.W.

It is the best word picture of ducks that I have ever read, rich in notan, rhythm, iridescent colour, duckly-awkward grace & valiancy. There is a pang in its humour & depth in its philosophy.

This poem appears in a little book GLOUCESTERSHIRE by F. W. Harvey Oliver & Boyd London: 98 Great Russell St. W.C., England.

I wish that I could send you a copy. It is a VISIT to the English countryside, with its people, horses, food, loves, & philosophy, in word pictures from the sparkling pen of a great poet of our time.

LOVE·FOR·MY·FRIENDS is worked in to every inch of this greeting for YOU!

Frances H. Bacheler

Harvey's poem "Ducks" used to decorate a Christmas card sent by a Frances Bacheler to her friends.

By courtesy of Mr Brian Frith

I

From troubles of this world
I turn to ducks,
Beautiful comical things
Sleeping or curled
Their heads beneath white wings
By water cool,
Or finding curious things
To eat in various mucks
Beneath the pool,
Tails uppermost, or waddling
Sailor-like on the shores
Of ponds, or paddling
—Left! right!—with fanlike feet
Which are for steady oars
When they (white galleys) float
Each bird a boat
Rippling at will the sweet
Wide waterway ..
When night is fallen you creep
Upstairs, but drakes and dillies
Nest with pale water-stars,
Moonbeams and shadow bars,
And water lilies:
Fearful too much to sleep
Since they've no locks
To click against the teeth
Of weasel and fox.
And warm beneath
Are eggs of cloudy green
Whence hungry rats and lean
Would stealthily suck
New life, but for the mien,
The bold ferocious mien
Of the mother-duck.

II

Yes, ducks are valiant things
On nests of twigs and straws,
And ducks are soothy things;
And lovely on the lake
When that the sunlight draws

And as for the duck, I think God must have smiled a bit
Seeing those bright eyes blink on the day He fashioned it.
And He's probably laughing still at the sound that
            came out of its bill![1]

Years later an American woman used this poem to decorate the Christmas greetings card which she sent to her friends and added,

"It is the best word picture of ducks that I have ever read, rich in notan, rhythm, iridescent colour, duckly-awkward grace and valiancy. There is a pang in its humour and depth in its philosophy. This poem appears in a little book *Gloucestershire* by F.W. Harvey, Oliver & Boyd, London, 28 Great Russell Street, WC England. I wish that I could send you a copy. It is a VISIT to the English countryside, with its people, horses, food, loves and philosophy, in word pictures from the sparkling pen of a great poet of our time.

LOVE-FOR-MY-FRIENDS is worked in every inch of this greeting for You!
Frances H. Bacheler."

The last tragic blows of the war for Harvey were the deaths of his two brothers. Bernard was the youngest, and his military service had been deferred so that he could run the farm. At the age of nineteen he was killed in a motorcycle accident on Over bridge.

Then, in the last week of the war, his brother Eric, with whom he had always had a close relationship, and who had studied theology at Oxford and was to go into the church, was killed in France.

It was not until the spring of 1919 that Harvey returned to England, and as the train bearing him drew nearer home he watched eagerly for his first sight of the dear, familiar scenery.

> The golden fields wheel round —
>   Their spokes, green hedges;
> And at the galloping sound
>   Of the train, from watery sedges
>   Arise familiar birds.
>
> Pools brown, and blue, and green,
>   Criss-crossed with shadows,
> Flash by, and in between
>   Gloucestershire meadows
>   Lie speckled red with herds.

---

[1] "Ducks", *Ducks and Other Verses*, Sidgwick & Jackson, 1919, p. 13.

A little flying farm,
   With humped grey back
Against the rays that warm
   To gold a last-year stack,
      Like a friendly cat appears,

And so through gloom and gleam
   Continues dwindling,
While in my heart a dream
   Of home awakes to kindling
      Fire and falling tears.[1]

Of his homecoming he wrote, "It is wonderful to get home — home: in the grave beauty of night to lie wakeful, disturbed only by the delicious unrest of the trees — kept awake, as by a lover, all night. It is happiness. There is the moonlight cold and quiet, and bars of darkness within the room; and outside in the whiteness of moonshine my dear hills, so blue, phantom-fast and shadowy — the hills that I shall see again (and so changed) at dawn. . . . Now at last I am in my own country and in my own county. I don't care if I never leave either again."[2]

[1] "Gloucestershire from the Train", *Farewell*, Sidgwick & Jackson, 1921, p. 26.
[2] *Comrades in Captivity*, Chapter the Last, Sidgwick & Jackson, 1920.

Return to Reality

For some time after he returned from the war Harvey was convalescing at the family home in Minsterworth. Physically and mentally he was at a low ebb. He was suffering from the after-effects of a bad attack of jaundice which he had developed in one of the camps, and his inner reserves had been drained by his efforts to rise above the prison camp mentality.

All those who knew him found him greatly changed. He was haunted by his experiences in the trenches and felt that he owed a debt to those, many of them boyhood friends, who had been killed. But whatever he wrote seemed quite inadequate to express the enormity of the suffering which he had witnessed.

> Words for what you think,
> Words for what you have seen,
> Words! Can I make them cry, and bleed, and stink;
> Turn them to flesh that's green?[1]

However, the War Office had not quite finished with him. In letters to Miss Marion Scott, in March and April 1919, Ivor Gurney wrote:

"F.W.H is all too soon to be back at Seaton Delaval, alas! ... He has just done 3 ripping poems on 'Coal', 'Iron' and 'Fire' ..."

"...Alas, Will Harvey is at Seaton Delaval! Disgusted to go, but the War Office had lost sight of him and he must be rescued from the pigeon holes. When I go to the Redlands however, I will ask about the new poems. There is a glorious Ballade of Leeuwarden and a Drinking Song good enough for anything."[2]

At last the War Office released Harvey; he received his demobilisation papers and arrived back among his beloved hills, to which he turned for strength and comfort. These hills possess certain qualities which had inspired Harvey since early childhood. They are large, but not majestic, rolling, but not awe-inspiring; they are big and warm and comfortable, glorious yet homely. Harvey had come to believe that they embodied reality. This feeling grew so strong in him that he wrote:

---

[1] "Words", *Ducks and Other Verses*, Sidgwick & Jackson, 1919, p. 77.
[2] The Ivor Gurney Archive, Gloucester City Library.

"Christian teaching in no way shook my childish preconceived conviction, but strengthened it. The part in all the Bible which I most liked, which was 'realest' to me was the Revelation with its horses, its fruit trees, its streams of water, the glorious city and its inhabitants, spiritualised all into Reality.

"I did not then know any more of England than a few miles surrounding the city of Gloucester, but it sufficed. There were the horses, there the waters of Severn, the men, the trees and the city, the unrealised country of God!"[1]

By degrees Harvey recovered his spirits and renewed his friendships with those who had returned from the war and formed new ones with many more who came under the spell of his rich and lovable personality.

He would tramp along the Gloucester roads and climb the hills, his favourite being May Hill, where he would go to watch the sun set in a great ball of fire. On his return journey he would stop at the Red Lion at Huntley, calling to the landlord, "Bill Harry, bring me more of your oldest beer in one of your largest tankards — and if there is one who would care to drink with me, why, bring him the same and we will sit down together."

Then, when he had had enough of singing old songs and drinking old beer, he would return home again.[2]

In May 1919 Ivor Gurney went to stay with the Harveys. He was displaying signs of the mental instability which was later to overcome him completely, but for the time he was happy to share his friend's contentment to be back in Gloucestershire. As he wrote to Marion Scott:

"No, there is no chance of F.W.H. being in London as far as I know — he is too stuck at home, too happy there, especially now the blossoms are coming on.

"He is contemplating a new book this Autumn, which will have some rattling good stuff therein. As to sales, *A Gloucestershire Lad* is now in the 5th edition, a remarkable thing.

"He is becoming his jolly old self once more and will no doubt grow completely into the F.W.H. of old cricket and haymaking days. ...

"Mr Haines told me *War's Embers* [Gurney's book of poems] was announced this week or last so soon the critics will be red of fang and happy. F.W.H. is to review it in the *Gloucester Journal*."[3]

Once it was learned that Harvey had returned, he was much in

---

[1] "Patriotism", *The Gloucester Journal*, 22.4.22.
[2] *Comrades in Captivity*, Sidgwick & Jackson, 1920.
[3] The Gurney Archives, Gloucester City Library.

demand to give recitals of his poetry, some of which his friend set to music.

In 1919 John Haines wrote to Marion Scott:

"...F.W. Harvey gave a poetry recital at Stroud on Saturday and it was illustrated by several songs set by Gurney and accompanied by him."[1]

But the main task which Harvey had set himself in those months after his return was to write a book of his experiences in seven German prison camps, entitled *Comrades in Captivity*. In it he set out, not only his experiences, but also many of his beliefs and ideals. The inspiration which he had received from his comradeship with men of all backgrounds was still with him and it fired him to complete the book within a year. It was published by Sidgwick & Jackson in 1920 and dedicated to "Old Gefangener Friends, but particularly to the PT and to my friend Ivor Gurney".[2]

Unfortunately the book was published too soon after the war when people were trying to forget all that had happened to them; there was a reaction against anything which might remind them of their experiences, and it was not a success.

Like many of his fellows, Harvey had returned home full of hope for the future, for the New England which they hoped would emerge when their efforts to preserve freedom had borne fruit.

> We died (whatever lie be spun)
> Less for "old England" than, each one,
> For the New England which shall shed
> Her sorrows, walking diamonded
> With love to praise Love's sweetest Son . . .
>   Will ye forget?[3]

In a note from the book of poems from which the above is taken, he wrote:

"What England needs is a spiritual ideal. . . . In pocket we, like every other European nation are poorer than before.

"We have gained only in national experience, and now is the time to invest it.

"A comradeship of ghastly experience knits up all classes.

"Now is the time to reconstruct; to understand; to get unity of aim; to fashion a New England."[4]

---

[1] The Gurney Archives, Gloucester City Library.
[2] *Comrades in Captivity*, Sidgwick & Jackson, 1920.
[3] "The Dead Speak", *Ducks and Other Verses*, Sidgwick & Jackson, 1919, p. 89.
[4] id., p. 73

Harvey had always had a respect for his fellow men, whatever their position in life and this had increased during his imprisonment. He was aware that changes in the way of life in England would be inevitable after the war, but he appealed to the employers (recently officers) and to the labourers (lately "the ranks") to remember how well they had worked together during the war, when they had a common aim, so that when trouble arose in civilian life, the employers should resist the temptation to call the workers "lazy scoundrels" or "ignorant agitators", and the workers should recall that these "hateful and greedy capitalists" were once leaders whom they trusted. He concluded:

"The solution of the labour difficulty will doubtless lie in a *common* ideal. Perhaps the politicians will supply it."[1]

When John Haines discovered that Harvey was continuing to write, he tried to encourage him to widen his circle of literary acquaintances and took him to see John Masefield who was then living at Boar's Hill, as also were Robert Graves and Robert Bridges.

Robert Bridges took an interest in Harvey's work for some years and of *Comrades in Captivity* he wrote, "Your book has a secure place on my shelves and it has helped me to think more kindly of the Germans."

He also greatly admired Harvey's poem "Ghosts" and on his insistence Harvey altered the wording in the third verse of the original.

Harvey was an admirer of the poet A.E. Housman and once said, "A Gloucestershire Lad would probably never have been born, had it not been for another lad, and better, from Shropshire."[2]

However, although he once visited W.H. Davies when that poet was living at Nailsworth, Harvey never made any real effort to keep in personal touch with contemporary poets and writers.

When he was fit enough to resume his former occupation, he took a position with a firm of solicitors in Swindon, but he was not happy to be away from his beloved county.

While he was there he jotted down some of his thoughts on his occupation as a solicitor.

"I have been picked to play the law game — to field slip. It is not bad fun and less running to do than at long field. I will play. But I will not forget the Realities. ... Law is a tricky business and my office hours are crammed with excitement now that I have been out of it for six years

---

[1] *Comrades in Captivity*, Sidgwick & Jackson, 1920, ch. IV, Men and Books.
[2] Lecture on Modern Poetry by F.W.H. at Gloucester Girls' High School, reported in the *Gloucester Journal*, 14.5.21.

and forgotten the little I did once know. The bluff required is abnormal and one is constantly having the 'wind put right up' one by the sudden discovery that something most essential to procedure has been overlooked and that there may or may not be *just* time to conform to precedent which has no care for ex-warriors."[1]

At one point he returned home to enter a nursing home for an operation on a gland, and it is said that it was there that he met the woman who was to become his wife. She was an Irish nurse and Harvey had always been fascinated by the Irish. He told someone that he fell in love with her voice and her gentleness. He may also have been attracted to her because she shared his disregard for the material things of life; she had been brought up to accept an uncomplicated and simple existence. As Harvey was already a convert to Roman Catholicism they shared the same faith, and Harvey once wrote, "It is not good for man to live alone, especially in belief."[2]

However, his family was not happy about the match; they felt that the two came from such different backgrounds, and at that time this was considered to be a great disadvantage to a marriage. Will and Anne were finally married very quietly at the church of the Holy Rood, Swindon, on 30th April, 1921. Of the event Ivor Gurney wrote to Miss Scott,

"Will Harvey is getting married! Quite suddenly, to all his friends. A Miss Kane. She's very nice and very Irish. They'll be happy.

"Pity it's Swindon though!

"Well, so things go."[3]

The same year that he was married, Harvey published another book of poems entitled *Farewell* which contained the following enigmatic preface:

"In spite of all the soulful utterances of people comfortably off, economic independence remains the first condition of happiness.

"This is not to say that people aren't great fools for preferring law to literature. It is rather to imply that a poet who can do both is a fool if *he* does not.

I am not a fool.

Farewell!"[4]

It is not clear whether he was declaring publicly his intention to make a genuine effort to succeed in his legal career, having realised that

---

[1] Harvey's Scrapbook, Gloucester County Record Office.
[2] *Comrades in Captivity*, Sidgwick & Jackson, 1920, ch. IV.
[3] Letter from Ivor Gurney to Miss M. Scott, 19.4.21. Gurney Archives, Gloucester City Library.
[4] "Preface", *Farewell*, Sidgwick & Jackson, 1921.

with the responsibilities of marriage, he must try to make a reasonable living from it.

The reviewer of the book for the *Gloucester Journal* was mystified and wrote,

"... One hopes that the only significance the title bears is that it happens to be the last word in the few lines of his preface. It can scarcely be that he intends, like Prospero, henceforth to abjure the muse 'And deeper than ever did plummet sound' bury his book. Rather is the inference to be drawn from the somewhat enigmatical preface, preferring literature to the law, the farewell is to the latter.

"The same characteristics mark this volume as are to be found in its predecessors. While ranging over a variety of subjects, he turns again and again to Gloucestershire as to his alma mater, and it is here that he is at his best. There is a ring of absolute sincerity in these poems...

"The volume is, however, a valuable contribution to the poetry of the county and it is not too much to hope that in the future Mr. Harvey will do for Gloucestershire what Mr. Kipling and Mr. Hilaire Belloc have done for Sussex."[1]

In another local paper the reviewer wrote:

"The young poet should be an experimentalist, anxious to advance the horizon of his craft; yet in the end he must depend on his experience of life, and returning to the country of his first and last love, confess with the Cornish singer:

'The land that did make shall take and show me
    Better than I have seemed to be.'

"Better, that is to say, not only as man but also as poet. Mr. Harvey is most himself when he shakes the grey dust of city streets off his shoes and decides to go back to the only shire worth living in."[2]

Harvey must have had a previous title, dedication and preface for the book, because a copy of the final one appears in his scrapbook with the note:

"(cut out original preface and all dedication)
New Title 'Farewell!' "[3]

He and his wife remained in Swindon in rooms for a time, but he was impatient all the while to return "home" and eventually he obtained a position with John Haines in Gloucester.

---

[1] *The Gloucester Journal*, 3.5.21.
[2] Local paper, Tuesday, May 2nd, 1921.
[3] Harvey's Scrapbook, Gloucester County Record Office.

He and Anne lived at The Redlands at Minsterworth while they looked for a home of their own. It was not an easy arrangement for Anne, for she came in for a certain amount of criticism from various members of the family and Mrs Harvey was only too happy to have Will in her care again.

The musical gatherings were resumed and once, at the end of a particularly successful evening, Mrs Harvey put her arm round her son's shoulder and said to the lingering guests, "You don't mind if I have Will to myself for a little while do you?"

Finally friends offered them a week-end cottage in the middle of the woods at Cranham, and his sister went with them to help to arrange things. The situation was ideal for both of them, for neither hankered after any refinements, and although the cottage offered only the bare essentials, Anne was quite happy to take every day as it came, washing the clothes in a stream if need be and hanging them on the bushes to dry. Harvey walked into Gloucester every day and so had time to draw inspiration from the surrounding countryside.

> Because I loved with deep desire,
> Wooing all as I walked,
> This noble country by tree and spire
> Taught (as if music talked)
> How Beauty is never bought or sold,
> But freely given to them
> Who worship more than crowns of gold
> Her dew-bright diadem.[1]

In 1922 Harvey's happiness was clouded by the news that his old friend Ivor Gurney had finally succumbed to the insanity which had been threatening for years, and that he had been sent to Barnwood House, a private asylum on the edge of Gloucester. Shortly after being admitted, Gurney attempted to escape and while out wrote some letters by which his mentor, Miss Marion Scott, learned of the escapade. She had obviously written a letter of annoyance to Harvey to which he replied:

"Thank you for your letter. *Of course* we are *always* pleased to answer any enquiries. I myself should have informed you of the 'escape' had I known that Ivor had written any letters during his absence from BH. but no good seemed likely to result from alarming his friends needlessly.

---

[1] "On Birdlip", *Farewell*, Sidgwick & Jackson, 1921, p. 16.

"As the telephone may or may not have made clear, he *was* safely back again by 3 o'clock the same afternoon.
                              "Yours very sincerely,

                                                    F.W. Harvey.

"P.S. I'm afraid that there is little, if any, mental improvement; but perhaps we can scarcely expect that yet. At any rate, he is having the best possible chance."[1]

Harvey was greatly troubled by his friend's incarceration in a mental hospital. Remembering how much it had meant to him to wander freely through the Gloucestershire lanes and to share his thoughts with someone of like mind, he dedicated a poem to him.

> This hawthorn hedge will bank its snow
>   Spring after Spring, and never care
> What song and dreams of long ago
>   Within its shade were fashioned fair
>   Of happy air.
>
> But you within the madhouse wall,
>   But you and I who went so free,
> Never shall keep Spring's festival
>   Again, though burgeon every tree
>   With blossom joyously.[2]

Marion Scott was obviously aware of Harvey's sadness at the physical and mental change in his old friend and in March 1928 she wrote to him:
    "Today I have sent off a packet to you. It contains a photograph of a picture of the young Schubert, but when you see it I think you will feel, as I do, that it might almost as well have been a picture of the young Ivor. I had a copy of it given to me as a present by Miss Fanny Davies, (the pianist) and I begged her while she was in Vienna this month to get me one or two more copies. It is one of these that I am sending after having had it framed. I thought you might like to have it for a remembrance of Ivor as he was . . ."[3]

---

[1] Letter from F.W.H. to Miss Scott, 21.10.22. Ivor Gurney Archives, Gloucester City Library.
[2] "To Ivor Gurney", *Gloucestershire*, Oliver & Boyd, 1947, p. 30.
[3] Letter from Miss Marion Scott to F.W.H. The Gloucester Collection, Gloucester City Library.

Later in the same year Harvey's spirits were lifted again by the birth of his daughter Eileen, who was to bring him much joy.

In his spare time Harvey had reformed the football team at Minsterworth and also continued to play hockey, becoming a member of the Gloucester Thursday Hockey Club, whose president was his employer and friend John Haines.

Harvey was once called upon to defend the Gloucester hockey players who were prosecuted at Pershore for drinking before the appointed hour. In court he pointed out that as the Pershore players (who had already finished their drinks when the law-breaking was discovered) were allowed to go free, it was hardly fair that the Gloucester men, who were "slower on the bend" should have to suffer! In spite of the amusement caused by this ingenious effort on Harvey's part, the magistrates were not persuaded by his argument.[1]

Working in an office in the city was not an ideal position for Harvey; he had once referred to towns as "These ulcers of civilisation"[2] and he was always glad to get back to the peace of the countryside.

> Here in the ring of the hills,
>   Under a cloudy sky,
>   Content at last I lie
> Where Peace o'erspills
>   Like a cool rain which giveth
> This brave daisy scent
> And wine of sacrament
>   Whereby he liveth.[3]

Perhaps John Haines sensed Harvey's need, for when he opened an office in the picturesque village of Newnham-on-Severn, he offered him the post of Managing Clerk. This was an opportunity to get back to the part of Gloucestershire which was most familiar to him, and much as he loved the cathedral there, nevertheless, Gloucester *was* a city, and Harvey was a countryman at heart.

---

[1] Letter from Mr. W. B. Cornock to the Gloucester paper, 1957.
[2] *Comrades in Captivity*, Sidgwick & Jackson, 1920, ch. IV.
[3] "Out of the City", *Farewell*, Sidgwick & Jackson, 1921, p. 17.

The Poet's Roots

In 1923 an American from the city of Gloucester, Massachusetts, visited Gloucester, England, and on his return produced an article for his local *Daily Times*. In it he wrote:

"Gloucestershire, the fertile, western county of England whose cathedral city gave our seaport its name three centuries ago, is fortunate in the possession of a poet of its own. Mr. F.W. Harvey belongs to Gloucestershire as truly as Professor Housman to Shropshire. One of the many young Englishmen in whom the war made the love of country articulate, and who found expression for it in verse, he is one of the few who today keep the title of poet. ...

"The wide appeal of Mr. Harvey's poetry is perhaps chiefly due to his passionate love of nature, born of close intimacy and rooted in familiar places...

"There is a strange power in names. To detect any resemblance between our Gloucester moors and the orcharded English Gloucestershire that stretches from the Cotswold hills to the Severn would be a difficult task. Yet — or so it seems to one who not many months ago journeyed from this Gloucester to the other — whatever belongs to the English countryside about the cathedral city of Gloucester has, if only for the name's sake, a claim of interest upon our western city by the sea. A Gloucestershire poet should therefore not be without honour among readers in American Gloucester."[1]

As a result of this article, an American wrote to Harvey asking him what had influenced him most in writing poetry. He replied:

"God originated it all, using many channels such as a loving father and mother, brothers, sister, friends, and breeding in an English County home — a farm in Gloucestershire where I first saw the ducks, although 'Ducks' (the poem) resulted more than twenty years later, drawn upon the walls of a German prison cell.

"God gives all. Poets patiently prepare themselves for the inspiration so not lazily to employ the sacred gift. That's all."[2]

When Harvey took up his new post at Newnham, he rented a pair of

[1] *The Gloster Citizen*, 22.9.23.
[2] *The Gloster Citizen*, 22.9.23.

converted railway carriages on the banks of the Severn at Broadoak —
and here, among the orchards, the fertile valley and the surrounding
hills and woods he "employed his sacred gift".

In fact Harvey was almost obsessed by a belief in the influence of
roots and native soil. The world existed on a lesser scale for him
outside his own county and this was reflected in his poetry, to the
extent that it earned him the unofficial title of The Poet Laureate of
Gloucestershire. He watched every sign of growth and change as the
months and seasons of the year came and went; he learned to recognise
the signs of the seasons when they were imperceptible to others.

> Spring came by water to Broadoak this year.
>   I saw her clear.
> Though on the earth a sprinkling
> Of snowdrops shone, the unwrinkling
> Bright curve of Severn River
> Was of her gospel first giver.[1]

His love of the country and his religious belief became intertwined as
he recognised spiritual qualities in nature. In his poem "On Wintry
Hedges" he conveyed the mystery of spring breaking the bonds of
winter's apparent death. Harvey saw that in the country there seemed
to be a constant death and resurrection from one season to another.
While mourning the tragedy of the dying summer, autumn entered
with its sharp, nostalgic beauty:

> She walketh like a ghost,
>   Lovely and gray
> And Faint, faint, faint . . .
>   Ere Autumn's host
> Of colours gay
>   Breaks on the year, September
> Comes sighing her soft pliant,
>   "Remember!"[2]

To the end of his life Harvey never lost his sense of wonder in
creation. He once said, "Wonder is the root of wisdom and the root of
poetry — it is the root of everything."

Eventually, the poet and lover of nature in him began to dominate
his Catholic faith, the discipline of the Catholic ritual was a restraint

---

[1] "Spring 1924", *September and Other Poems*, 1925.
[2] "September", *September and Other Poems*, 1925

and he felt the need to be free to find God in natural things, to worship him through his senses and his emotions. His creed was based on a faith in nature, and like the pantheists he found God in all creation.

> This Sunday morning
> I will not go to Mass.
> I will not do anything
> But lie in the grass
> And watch the great clouds pass;
> Moving with a slow majesty
> And peace unknown, high, high,
> Above the world of men and church bells calling.[1]

As he worked among them and shared their problems, Harvey grew to admire and to love the county people of the Severn valley. He had always been fascinated by their quaint turn of phrase and the picturesque way in which they expressed themselves. He compared their speech with that of Shakespeare and Chaucer, saying that their limited vocabulary had resulted in the invention of words to express what they wanted to say.

It is said that many of the terms and phrases in use in the Gloucestershire dialect may be found in the works of Shakespeare, perhaps one of the reasons why Harvey felt such an affinity with him.

In fact the influence of the Gloucestershire dialect on Shakespeare was referred to by a Rev. Richard Huntley, writing in 1868, who had a theory that Shakespeare had taken shelter in the county during his flight from Warwickshire, on his way to London, and had stayed at Woodmancot in the parish of Dursley, where later a popular walk became known as Shakespeare Walk.[2]

In any case, Harvey admired Shakespeare tremendously and frequently read him and quoted from his work. Once, when a comparison was made between them both he replied humbly, "To compare Will Shakespeare with me is like comparing Gloucester Cathedral with a prefab."

The true Gloucestershire dialect is dying out, but the native speech of the district remains strong in the Severn Valley and it is this which was reproduced by the poet.

The keynote of all Harvey's dialect poetry is simplicity, the simplicity of the country people. Yet this does not imply that they are

---

[1] "Clouds", *Ducks and Other Verses*, Sidgwick & Jackson, 1919, p. 48.
[2] Rev. R.W. Huntley, *A Glossary of the Cotswold (Gloucestershire) Dialect*.

Top: In the early days of their marriage, Will and Anne lived in a cottage in Cranham Woods.
Bottom: The Severn in flood – a familiar scene in Will's childhood.

By courtesy of Miss Frances Eacott

Mrs. Harry, wife of the landlord of The Red Lion, Huntley. Harvey's long country walks ended here during his period of rehabilitation after release from German prison camp.

Top: May Hill – one of
Harvey's favourite walks as a
young man.

Bottom: Hawthorn hedges – a
reminder of Harvey's happy
association with Ivor Gurney.
*By courtesy of Miss Frances
Eacott*

The unveiling of the F.W. Harvey memorial plaque by Lt./Col. H.L.T. Radice in Gloucester Cathedral, March 1980.
By courtesy of the Gloucester Journal and Citizen

without sense, far from it. They are shrewd and wise; their wisdom is gained by their experience and by studying all the natural things around them.

In the group of dialect poems which Harvey wrote, one finds those facets which, when fitted together, form the whole crystal of life. What could be more simple than this country love song?

> The days between the days we meet
>   What be um more than shadows —
> Like the strong zun do cast along
>   From elms over the meadows?
>
> Those days whereon we meet, my sweet,
>   Being zuns both bright and strong,
> Make in their rays all other days
>   Fall just zo black and long![1]

The countryman's philosophy is bound up with his practical needs, and the expression of his feelings and emotions shows this:

> We heard as we wer passing by the forge:
>   " 'Er's dead," said he.
> " 'Tis Providence's doing," so said George.
> "He's allus doing summat," so I said,
> "You see this pig; we kept un aal the year
> Fatting un up and priding in un, see,
> And spent a yup o' money — food so dear!
>   I wish 'twer 'e;
> I'd liefer our fat pig had died than she."[2]

It is Gloucestershire's loss that Harvey did not write more dialect poems, for not only would they have put him in the same class as the Dorset poet Barnes, but also they would have been a valuable social document.

In 1925 Harvey again had cause for joy and for disappointment. His second child, Patrick, was born and later his most important book of poetry, *September and Other Poems*, was published. It was entered the same year as a candidate for the Hawthornden Prize and it was a great blow to him when it was not chosen.

He had no patience with fashions in poetry and he did not like the

---

[1] "Country Love Song", *September and Other Poems*, 1925.
[2] "Seth bemoans the Oldest Inhabitant", *Gloucestershire Friends*, Sidgwick & Jackson, 1917, p. 52.

way in which Art and Literature were developing, but he was convinced that one day people would return to his style of writing.

Some years after the war Harvey had been invited to speak at the Gloucester Girls' High School on modern poetry and he told his audience that English verse was not to be regarded as a bundle of sticks picked up in a forest of books, but, in its lusty youth, as in its venerable age, as a lovely and living tree. If modern poetry was, in essence, different from that which had gone before it, then it was not poetry. He asserted that poetry must follow the forms and principles which had governed it from the beginning, that it was not possible to make a poem, apart from obedience to the principles of writing.[1]

F.W. Baty, the author of *The Forest of Dean*, recalling Harvey's attendance at meetings of the Gloucester Writers' Circle, said that he once urged members to look at poetry, like stained glass, from the inside towards the light.

He gave it as his view that a poet could only be said to have "arrived" when six of his poems were widely known, and he claimed only three. When asked which two made up the trio with "Ducks" he replied, "That is for each one of you to decide."

In 1926 Frank Harris of Lydney produced another small volume of Harvey's poems entitled *In Pillowell Woods*. In the preface Harvey wrote:

"These poems, mostly of an occasional order, have been collected into book form at the suggestion and with the encouragement of Mr. Frank Harris, who must take the responsibility. Lest you should (with memories of Dickens) think that there is 'no sich person', I have asked him to write a few notes where such seem necessary, to explain local references, upon which subject he is a recognised authority.

"Without any clear-cut division the book arranges itself under three heads, viz.:

Nature Poems: ...
Poems written for public occasions: ...
Religious Poems: ...

"There is also (consisting of only two poems) a *Bucolic Section*. Local opinion being not undivided with regard to the subject matter, which is the desirability of drinking beer, these two poems are printed on one page, which can easily be excised with a scissors or safety-razor blade without detriment to the remaining portion of the book. Thus a sort of local option may be exercised."

In a letter, Harvey had once written that his favourite occupation

---

[1] *Gloucester Journal*, May 14th, 1921.

was "drinking beer and listening to Gloucestershire stories" and maintained that all good poems were born in pubs.

Although Harvey's work was not included in most of the Georgian anthologies, his poetic talent was recognised by Humbert Wolfe, the editor of *The Augustan Books of Modern Poetry*, a series which was to include every major poet, living or dead. A collection of his work was published in this series in 1926, containing thirty-one poems. The introduction declared that "Mr. Harvey's poetry found an immediate welcome, especially in his own county, Gloucestershire."

Independence and Disillusionment

Harvey still found the routine work of a solicitor's office irksome and he did not enjoy taking instructions from other people. He longed to be independent, to be free to choose his own cases and perhaps to have more time for his writing. He finally decided to set up in practice on his own and rented an office adjoining Old Bank House in the High Street in Lydney. The contract was signed in spring 1925 when Harvey agreed to rent the office from 1st May for five years at a rent of £30 per annum. At the end of this time he moved to other premises near the post office.

His poetic outlook on life immediately became evident in his office, whose walls he hung with pictures of great composers. His first piece of furniture, an office desk, set him thinking of the beauties of the furniture, an office desk, set him thinking of the beauties of the woodlands.

> Behold a fine
> New varnished desk, with nine
> Useful drawers, a slanted
> Surface, and pigeon-holes:—granted
> Well worth my five pounds ten.
> 'Tis oak. There's grain
> Under that yellow polish flowing clear
> Yet close.
> Oak. . . . Once did rain
> Patter in English woods on this severe
> Dead piece of usefulness: sap rose
> With blood's mysterious power;
> An April shower
> Made music on the leaves,
> Which after,
> Like eyes, shone with young laughter,
> Blinking at bluebells. . . . So
> Did not mine too?
> Ah, the Spring grieves
> Less o'er that tree
> Now but a lawyer's desk, than over *me*![1]

---

[1] "Office Furniture", *In Pillowell Woods*, Frank Harris, Lydney, 1926, p. 10.

Harvey was a great lover of trees and forests and was once grieved to find that inadvertently he had been responsible for the felling of several fine sycamores along the roadside. He had represented a motorist in court who had skidded on the wet road and Harvey had pleaded that this was due, not to the motorist's careless driving, but to the presence of sycamore seeds which had been pressed into a slippery pulp on the road's surface.[1]

The clerk at Haines and Sumner at Newnham-on-Severn had been persuaded to join Harvey in his venture. She was extremely efficient and well versed in all aspects of legal work, but unfortunately, although Harvey was a brilliant advocate, he was a hopeless businessman. He tried to avoid the more mundane work of a solicitor, which is his bread and butter, and took on only those cases which interested him. He always preferred to defend rather than to prosecute. He seemed to take a Quixotic pleasure in being the champion of the underdog and could reduce a court to tears by his eloquence and impassioned pleas for clemency. However, there was insufficient work of this kind in a country district to keep a solicitor secure financially, and for the rest, he had little patience. If there were Abstracts of Title and Conveyances to prepare, he would throw the papers onto his clerk's desk and say, "You know all about these, you can get on with them," for references to "parcels of land" would only set him thinking of blossom-laden orchards or fields golden with buttercups. Then he would retreat into his inner office into a world of dreams, thankful to leave the dull practicalities of his work in the hands of someone prepared to organise them for him. Occasionally his mother would come to the office to visit him, no doubt anxious about the way things were going, and on her way out she would say to the clerk, "Thank you for all you are doing for Will."

His friends often tried to put work his way, but if he did not find it interesting, he could not be bothered. Life, to him, did not consist of dry, legal points, but of beauty, music and fellowship. He quoted Morris's words, "Fellowship is life and lack of fellowship death." Therefore, he would go and seek it out, completely oblivious of the restrictions of routine and of the clock. When he went over to The Feathers at lunch-time, he was unaware of anything but the companionship of those he found there, seeking to recapture perhaps the camaraderie he had known in the army, standing rounds of drinks which he could ill afford, or being persuaded to go off to watch a cricket match.

---

[1] Letter to Gloucester paper, Mr Cornock, 1957.

Often his clerk had to telephone to The Feathers to remind him of an appointment with a client, and when at the office, he would frequently amble off, singing, his mind completely absorbed in his poetry. He was quite unable to carry out his affairs in a practical and business-like way, for he acted upon intuition rather than reason; he was more interested in men than in social principles.

The Forest of Dean was a great contrast to the Severnside area in which Harvey had been brought up. A strong Victorian attitude persisted for many years, the men still playing the dominant role, and there was a great respect for anyone who had received a good education.

During the 1920's and 30's there was mass unemployment in the Forest which created great poverty and hardship. Most of the men in the villages were miners, and their families lived in cramped conditions, in tiny cottages with no running water or indoor sanitation, no electricity or gas and without even a regular refuse collection. The only concessions these people received were an allowance of 12 hundred-weight of coal per month and the ancient rights of grazing their animals on the common land.

Malnutrition and tuberculosis were rife. For the old there was the dread of the workhouse and for the young the constant fear of having to seek medical aid which they could not afford. The death of a small child was not uncommon, and Harvey grieved with the families in their bereavement.

> This little girl
> In brown earth lies
> She shall sweeten the sweet air
> Of Paradise
> With her slow lovely speech
> And wondering eyes.[1]

The only pleasures which life provided for the menfolk of the families were tobacco and drink and they would gather in one of the many locals to enjoy these pleasures in the company of others, and it was here that Harvey would go to meet his friends, the Foresters, as he called them. He had great sympathy for the plight of the Forest people and believed that their economic conditions were the cause of many of their problems. He once wrote:

"If deliberation is the essence of crime, then I think we have *no* crime in the Forest of Dean.

---

[1] "Epitaph", *Gloucestershire*, Oliver & Boyd, 1947, p. 8.

"Offences against the person (hasty and in hot blood) may be committed: offences against property also. These latter may be largely accounted for by that sense of forest communism which history has done so much to promote. There is very little plotting in cold blood — I might, I think, say that there is none. ...

"Housing conditions have a great deal to do with this. Very small houses do not make for harmony, especially when occupied by very large families. Pit work is done in three 'shifts'. It would be hard to find a miner's cottage where someone was not sleeping after having worked all night...

"Matrimonial disagreements are also very largely due to economic conditions. It is so difficult to be saving *and* look attractive ... the home, small as it is, is as a rule spotlessly clean — and this in spite of the dirt brought into it, for only one colliery in the district boasts pithead baths."[1]

Harvey became known in the Forest for his generosity and compassion and he was a man generous to the point of foolishness; as soon as he had money, he parted with it. If he felt a man could not afford to pay him a fee for his services he would often say, "Oh, never mind! Buy me a drink next time you see me."

No-one who had spent some time in Harvey's company could fail to be affected by his courteous manner, his gentleness and above all his sense of humour, which was always waiting to break through to the surface. He had an immense capacity for seeing the funny side of a situation and even for being able to laugh at himself. During his legal career he often provoked the courts to laughter. Someone once said of him, "When he laughed, he threw back his head, opened his toothless mouth and chuckled like a delighted little goblin."

When he was in a hilarious mood he could reduce his listeners (and himself) to helpless mirth. He had a most expressive face and was a talented mimic, but his laughter was never cruel, he was essentially humorous rather than witty and he differentiated between wit and humour in a chapter of his book *Comrades in Captivity*.

"Wit is mainly intellectual, but humour of the immortal spirit. . . . of the two, humour is the much more desirable gift of God. . . . One sees it in people's eyes, but chiefly in their conduct towards life. . . . I believe that its dominating note is courage. Its courage derives out of a sense of the final invincibility of the soul, and comes out of a deep, though often unconscious belief, as well as from a certain abstraction from worldly affairs. . . .

---

[1] "My Friends the Foresters", *Gloucestershire Countryside*, July 1936.

"Humour is wonderfully sane, it is a cooling medicine for all the fevers of life. Humour is a passionate, laughing impulse of the soul which saves men from committing suicide by preventing them from ever despairing. A man might commit suicide very wittily, it might well be the wittiest thing he ever did; but he could not do it humorously. . . . Wit flashes out occasionally but best in prosperity. Humour shines always, but most clearly in adversity. . . . Oh yes, there is a great deal of difference between the two."[1]

On the subject of humour he wrote once to someone:

"Comicality is as much an aspect of God as holiness. The fact that there are comical men and comical ducks proves that there is a comical God. One does not love one's Father any the less because one suspects Him of a sense of Humour."

This philosophy of Harvey's helps to explain his popularity with other men, for by it he helped many in unfortunate circumstances to keep their reason and to see things in perspective. To him, laughter and humour were a test of the faith of man; his faith in his fellows, in life and in God, and it was his sense of humour, combined with his compassion, which endeared him to the Foresters. Not only were others helped by his philosophy, but in the years to follow, Harvey was himself to test the truth of his belief.

He never owned a car and used to travel to court or to his office by bus or train. He knew the line from Lydney to Coleford well, and once, during a particularly slow journey, wrote a poem entitled "Lydney to Coleford (By Rail)".

Abandon hope all ye who here
　　Enter to keep appointment!
A gift more fair, a gift more rare,
　　A kind and healing ointment,
This train provides. Then cast away
Dull care, and for a Summer's day
Ignore as dross Time's "Yea" and "Nay",
　　Discard Life's fret and fear.

Too oft doth hurry rule us. Let
　　For once the tumult fade:
Fade into humming of bees coming
　　Sweet-laden down a glade:
Fade into glint of fern and flower,

[1] *Comrades in Captivity*, Sidgwick & Jackson, 1920, ch. 21.

Where quarries gleam and foxgloves tower,
And for one lovely lazy hour
  Forget — forget — forget.

You *will* arrive — impatient ass —
  Too soon! and then alighting
Meet kith and kin and wag a chin
  O'er wrongs past human righting.
Discuss old strife; new scandal: — such
Soft social soot as serves to smutch
A life once tuned to Nature's touch
  Now seldom felt — alas![1]

In a note at the end of the book in which this poem appeared, Harvey wrote:

'The following tale is told (with what truth I know not) by a popular Lydney innkeeper:

"One day I was in the bar-room when a man entered in an exhausted condition, sank into a seat, and called for a whiskey and soda.

"You look tired," I said.

"I've had an awful journey," he answered. *"Thank God the worst of it is over."*

"Come a long way?"

"From Coleford."

"And where might you be going?"

"To China," he replied.'[2]

On another occasion Harvey arrived at a village station after a tiring walk with some friends, to find that there was no train for several hours and that the lord of the manor on which the halt was situated would not allow a licensed house on his estate. Harvey sat in the waiting room and expressed his opinion of the said lord in verse. Apparently the original was not fit for publication, but was later revised and it appeared under the title "A Curse".

God burn this place called Soddington
  And tread it out to ashes,
And welt the slaves therein right sore
  With whips of many lashes.

But for the lord of Soddington,
  Who grudges men their beer,

---

[1] "Lydney to Coleford (By Rail)", *In Pillowell Woods*, Frank Harris, Lydney, 1926, p. 6.
[2] *In Pillowell Woods*, p. 31.

Let Satan hound him swift to hell
    With hot and pointed spear;

And ladle down his parching throat
    A quart of molten lead,
And heap the coals of Hades-fire,
    Blue hot upon his head.

And twist his thumbs, and pluck his beard,
    And rend him clean asunder,
And shrivel up his shrieking soul
    In brimstone and in thunder.[1]

In view of his unbusinesslike approach, it was hardly surprising that Harvey's practice began to go downhill and in the mid-1930's he sold out to a Chepstow firm of solicitors and carried on his work from his home, putting up a brass plate on his gate which read:

'F.W. Harvey, Solicitor and Commissioner for Oaths.'

He had made a number of moves after leaving Broadoak and had finally settled in the old School House in the village of Yorkley, a high, windswept area on the edge of the Forest, surrounded by common land. He felt a kind of affinity with the Forest people who are descended from an ancient Silurian tribe which originally occupied the area, a stubborn and independent race.

He became a familiar figure in his old trilby and shabby suit walking into Lydney to catch a train or bus to attend court, but unprepossessing though his appearance might have been, his eloquence in court became legendary and it was on this which he relied to win his cases. Rather than referring to books of law and past legal cases, he would turn to the Bible or to English Literature to support his defence of his client.

On one occasion he was defending a case at Gloucester City Quarter Sessions before the Recorder of Gloucester, Mr. Raglan Somerset K.C. who had a great feeling for the English language and had been a Classical Scholar at Cambridge. After the case had ended Harvey had returned to his seat, a small, bespectacled, somewhat unkempt-looking figure, clutching his papers with nicotine-stained fingers. Suddenly Mr. Somerset announced from the bench,

"Before the court proceeds to its next business, I wish to refer to the honour that has been bestowed on us today by the presence of that

---

[1] "A Curse", *In Pillowell Woods*, Frank Harris, Lydney, 1926, p. 29.

master of the King's English, Mr. Frederick Harvey," at which the poet's face broke into a beaming smile.

Harvey had always appreciated any kindness which he received, for it was a quality which he possessed in abundance. He once said,

"Kindness, (whether of God or of men) is the common air of the human heart, which dies without it. When a man feels that there is no kindness either in heaven above or on the earth beneath, he will commit suicide, and well he may, for he is already damned and dead."[1]

During the 1930's Harvey became disillusioned by the politicians; he felt betrayed and saddened by the standards which were respected in education and industry and by the belief in the survival of the fittest; he could not bear the self-promotion of national and local leaders. Although he did not hate these people, it was their principles and their actions which he loathed.

> I cannot get my heart to hate them!
> I know their thoughts are muddled and mad,
> Their motives mixed, their morals bad:
> That manifold small hells await them
> — Or should do if the devil had
> His due — but yet I cannot hate them![2]

Harvey lived among people who were oppressed by poverty, caught in the mesh of unemployment and debt, and his compassion reached out to them. It was to these humble people he finally turned for companionship, meeting them in the village pubs, trying to revive the spirit of comradeship he had once known.

Much of the time he would sit in a corner of the bar with a tankard of cider, listening to the discussions, most of them of a domestic or political nature, jotting down notes every now and then on the back of a used envelope.

Wherever he went the pockets of his shabby, ill-fitting overcoat bulged with books and often he would produce one of them and begin to read to the assembled company, casting a spell over his listeners with a voice that held them captivated, for he possessed an aura and a presence, like the sun which takes the light from the fire. He tried to introduce the heritage of English Literature to those who had been deprived of education and even as he wandered through the village, children would come running up to him and beg, "Give us a poetry Mr. 'arvey."[3] There were many young people in the Forest who owned their love of books to his encouragement.

---

[1] "Chapter the Last", *Comrades in Captivity*, Sidgwick & Jackson, 1920.
[2] "The Bad Men", *Ducks and Other Verses*, Sidgwick & Jackson, 1919, p. 83.
[3] Chapter X, *The Forest of Dean*, Brian Waters 1951.

Harvey believed that books contained the personalities of the men who wrote them. He said,

"I cannot help thinking of books as if they were men — and indeed, books are the flowers of a man's mind and exhale his essential odour."[1]

"If every book is in essence a man, so is every man a book — humorous, noble, fantastic, dirty as the case may be. And in the library of humanity there is no censor...

"Men, whether alive and veiled in the flesh, or dead and in books, are the proper study of mankind . . ."[2]

Harvey was a man deeply read in English literature but had little interest in the classics of Greece and Rome. While he was a prisoner-of-war he carried with him a copy of Shakespeare's sonnets and these gave him great pleasure, especially when he was in solitary confinement. Towards the end of his imprisonment in one of the last camps, he was reduced to reading a dictionary. As he said,

"I did it simply because I couldn't do anything else. It was so easy to stop when one wanted to and just dream ... picture after picture thrown upon the blank darkness of captivity by a Chambers Dictionary."[3]

Books were to Harvey more than food, they were the only possessions which he truly valued; they lined the walls or stood in piles on the floors of his house. They were worn and stained from constant handling and he would scribble notes in the margin or underline passages which he found of particular interest. He once said to a group of friends,

"Don't learn poetry by reading Chaucer and working your way to de la Mare. Start with de la Mare and read back to Chaucer. . . . Show me one of your modern poets and let me see him write a sonnet."[4]

Harvey had a great belief in the power of music to lift a man out of his surroundings, so he helped to found an annual music festival which took place in an atmospheric clearing in the Forest known as The Devil's Chapel. Here in ancient times there were iron pits worked first by the Silurians and then the Romans and it made a perfect setting. During the years of the depression he did all he could to encourage the Foresters' participation in playing and singing. He became a supporter of the Whitecroft Male Voice Choir, which was made up of about a

---

[1] Chapter XV, *Comrades in Captivity*, Sidgwick & Jackson, 1920.
[2] Chapter XV, *Comrades in Captivity*, Sidgwick & Jackson, 1920.
[3] Chapter XXVI, *Comrades in Captivity*, Sidgwick & Jackson, 1920.
[4] Obituary by Ivon Adams.

hundred men, most of them miners who somehow found the heart to sing. They always invited Harvey to their annual supper where he could be relied upon to make an entertaining speech.

On one occasion he began by apologising to his listeners for any difficulty which they might have in understanding him, as he was without dentures, which were new and had been causing him some problems. He remarked that all he had learnt from having all his teeth extracted and dentures fitted was that first impressions are not always the best! He never did become accustomed to wearing them and used to carry them around with him in his attaché case for use when he had to appear in court.

The composer Rutland Boughton went to listen to the men sometimes and he and Harvey arranged for the choir to broadcast, Harvey going with them to introduce the items. The party travelled by train and he would often turn up at the station at the last moment, unshaven and on one occasion wearing a battered panama hat which the men later threw out of the window.

When Viscount Bledisloe returned to Lydney after five years as Governor General of New Zealand, the schoolchildren of the town sang a Song of Welcome, with words written by Harvey and set to music by his friend Herbert Howells.

In 1937 his old friend, Ivor Gurney, died of consumption in a mental hospital in Dartford. It was some years since he had seen him, but the news affected him deeply and he felt that one more link with his carefree youth had been broken, for they had shared dreams and aspirations which had not been fulfilled. The realities of life had overtaken them and they had both become victims, not only of fate and circumstance, but of their temperaments.

Harvey's circumstances were far removed from those he had known as a boy and young man at Minsterworth. In a letter to their mutual friend, Brian Frith, in 1970 (thirteen years after Harvey's death) Herbert Howells wrote:

"Your letter about Gladys Harvey (in my mind she remained a 'Harvey') roused all sorts of memories of that remarkable house 'The Redlands' and the still more remarkable people who dwelt in it — and Gurney, and F.W.H. and the quintessential old Mrs. Harvey reigning over us all who used to find ourselves in her presence ... I wish I cd. rid my memory of his ...unhappy state of mind when he was in Pillowell and in the Lydney district — the happier days he spent at Minsterworth wd. be so much more worthy of being in one's recollection ... despite his path to Rome, I'm thinking Minsterworth was the most-loved resting place in his mind."

Indeed, a poem in *A Forest Offering* confirms this view of Howells:

I love old Minsterworth. I love the river
Where elver fishers bend with twinkling lights
And salmon catchers spend their fruitful nights.
I love the sleek brown skin, the mighty rush,
The angry head upreared, the splendid hush
When the Great Bore (grown breathless) 'ere he turns
Catches his wind; and nothing on the thick
Tide moves; and you can hear your watch's tick.[1]

Harvey was always ready to share what little he had with others. Once, when invited to a friend's wedding reception he was obviously distressed by the fact that he had not brought a gift. He slipped away for a while and returned with a dusty picture which he had removed from his wall — a picture which he had treasured since he brought it back from the war, entitled 'Sonntag' depicting three Ukrainian peasant women in Sunday best.

As a solicitor, Harvey would often take on an unpromising case. His clients trusted him and would walk many miles to see him. A man once walked in from Chepstow, joined the family for a meal, received his advice and returned home without making any payment. His ability to identify himself with all those whom he felt to be poor and oppressed by circumstance was remembered by a Forester in a radio programme about Harvey, who said that if he had a shilling in his pocket he would give 11½d of it away.[2]

Once when asked to collect a bad debt from someone in difficulties through no fault of their own he remarked,

"Money is not so important as human happiness."

Nevertheless, he was shrewd enough to know a scrounger when he met one. He once got the better of a crafty old Forester who had been taking advantage of his conversation with Harvey to ask him a number of questions about a certain problem that he had. When he had finished answering them all, Harvey said to the man,

"Now that will cost you 7/6 and I hope you are satisfied with the advice I have given you!"

Although he conducted his business from his home, Harvey never talked about his cases in front of the children who were sent from the room when a client arrived. He always insisted on complete discretion and confidentiality and although his wife stayed to help him to take notes, the children were always told,

"Anything you may hear spoken of in this house you never talk about outside."

---

[1] "My Village". *A Forest Offering.*
[2] B.B.C. broadcast "Will Harvey" August 1958 produced by Robert Waller.

The house to which the clients took their problems might have appeared bare and Spartan to those used to comfort. Nevertheless, the warmth of the welcome and the hospitality shown, made up for the lack of floor covering or curtains at the windows. The chickens accompanied one companionably into the house, the untrimmed branch which often stuck out across the hearth was pushed further into the grate, and at night a candle was lit and unceremoniously stuck into a pool of its own wax on the mantelpiece. One entered a house which had a curious sense of timelessness about it, for there was no clock of any kind, neither was there a radio or telephone.

To the Harveys many of the accepted conventions of daily life did not exist; to them the warmth of human friendship, loyalty and compassion were the important things, so that they appeared to be unaware of the practical details. The house was never locked; any caller was instructed to enter and Harvey found it unnecessary to explain or apologise when, on turning the handle one of his visitors was nonplussed to find that the door had come off its hinges and so fell into the passage. Harvey simply replaced the door in its frame and ushered the visitor in. If the guest was offered a drink, the glass was usually emptied of whatever was being stored in it, newspaper cuttings or perhaps hairgrips, before a drink was poured in.

Both Harvey and his wife seemed impractical in many ways, drifting from day to day, never living to an organised time-table and having a complete lack of interest in anything mechanical or labour-saving.

One Christmas-time he called on some friends just as they were about to start their meal and said,

"We've got a lovely turkey up there (each year he received a hamper from some relations) it's been cooking for several hours but one of the burners on the oil stove doesn't work, so we'll probably eat it this evening."

Another year Harvey won a large goose in a raffle which had been too large to fit into the stove, so he had tied the legs together and with the head still on it, had tried to hang it in the chimney over the open fire, but had not succeeded in anything more than singeing and blackening the bird. Finally he decided to take it to the village baker to have it cooked in one of his large ovens.

The plants in the garden were left to their natural tendencies, so that creepers covered the doors and twigs and branches grew across and even through the cracks in the window frames. On one occasion when the fire was getting low while Harvey had been talking to a visitor, he absentmindedly crossed the room, picked a few twigs which were poking through and put them onto the fire.

He had a preoccupation with the meaning of life and had no interest in the acquisition of material wealth or the ambitious striving for a position in society. His mode of living was a testimony to his belief. To the end of his life he and his family lived simply, without the so-called benefits of any modern electrical or mechanical inventions. His children grew up in an environment as materially poor as many of the Forest miners, but his riches were those which cannot be bought:

> Let me go lame and lousy like a tramp
>   But feel the wind and know the moonlit sky!
> What matter if the falling dew be damp —
>   Still is it dew! And well contented I
> Among my dreams (in seeming poverty).[1]

Although his childhood background had been one of a well-to-do farming family, where the house was solidly furnished and the table well-spread, he seemed to turn his back on all these refinements. The legacy left to him by his parents which he had cherished was that of education and breeding and he and his wife would try to impress the importance of these on their son and daughter. They were particular about the way the children spoke so that they found that they had to develop two modes of speech, one for use among the family and another among their peers.

When she was quite small, Harvey's daughter Eileen adopted an old man at Pillowell as her 'Grancher'; all the other children had one and she wanted one too. He used to give her strong tea to drink out of a saucer, which shocked her mother, and the child used to correct the old man's grammar when he sang the song, 'There 'ain't no sense, sittin' on a fence'.

It was perhaps natural that Harvey should feel an affinity with an old Mosaic figure in the Forest who carried on the trade of shoe-black and in consequence became known to the local people as 'Charlie the Black'. His real name was Edwin Ferris and he had come to the area from Exeter. He was a courteous and humble man with a well-bred voice and kindly manner. He used to travel the Forest on foot, shouldering his cumbersome box and sleeping where he could, in barns or outhouses or under hedges. At one time his shoe-cleaning outfit was stolen and he had no means of replacing it. Someone in the locality wrote to the Cherry Blossom factory to explain Charlie's plight and a new kit was provided free of charge. The presentation was made in one of the village pubs. and 'Charlie' was overwhelmed to have his means of livelihood restored to him.

---

[1] "Ballade of the Rich Heart", *A Gloucestershire Lad*, Sidgwick & Jackson 1918, p. 3.

He was said to have come from a good family and though his worldly goods were almost non-existent, he never refused to give to charity. Why he chose to lead such an eccentric life no-one knew or understood, except perhaps Harvey.

When 'Charlie' was found in a state of collapse in an outhouse he was removed to the local workhouse where he died. It was the men of the Whitecroft choir who paid for his body to be taken from the workhouse and be buried at Parkend. After his death Harvey was moved to write a poem about him, though with a touch of poetic licence he set the scene of 'Charlie's' death in a stable.

> Charlie "the black", and Christ, Our Lord,
> Lived lives that ran in strange accord:
> And spent them mostly on the road.
> . . . .
> Both country-lovers; both keen-eyed;
> Pondering oft through countryside
> How lambs and lilies lived and died.
>
> Christ washed the feet of disciples twelve,
> Charlie cleaned boots and shoes for pelf
> Enough (sometimes) to feed himself.
>
> Christ the King at Christmastide
> Was born in a stable with no pride.
> 'Twas in a stable Charlie died.[1]
> . . . .

During the thirty years that he lived in the Forest, Harvey came to realise how many of his fellows had never had the opportunity of an education such as he had received and his heart went out to those who lacked either education or intelligence.

> It's good to be born of wealthy stock and fed on healthy
> food,
> It's good to spend your strength, and sleep and wake with
> strength renewed:
> . . . .
> But it's exceeding evil to be ill-gotten and weak,
> With limbs unskilled to labour and tongue untrained to
> speak;
> With faint heart and feeble in a body puny and bad,
> And a whole world of brothers to bully and call you mad.[2]

---

[1] "Charlie the Black", *Gloucestershire*, Oliver & Boyd, 1957, p. 32.
[2] "The Contrast", *Ducks and Other Verses*, Sidgwick & Jackson, 1919, p. 81.

So Harvey constantly strove to fight against injustice and ignorance, often ignoring his own needs. His fellow solicitors came to his aid to try to help him out of his financial troubles, but he continued to live in the same way, till his body began to show signs of the deprivations to which it had been subjected, though his mind remained keen and alert.

The Final Years

After the outbreak of the Second World War, Harvey withdrew more and more into himself; he did not want to talk about war, for the subject was too painful for him.

An attempt was made by the re-formed 5th Glo'sters to start up another regimental *Gazette* and the first number contained an article by Harvey with the following introduction:

"The writer of the underwritten message and of other contributions to this Gazette, fought in the 5th Glo'sters during the war of 1914-1918 and was the chief contributor to the Old Gazette. He is justly famed as a poet and not only in his native Gloucestershire. We are proud to have his contribution to the first number of our revival, and although it is too much to hope that we shall find among us talent the equal of his, we have a fine example of his to strive to emulate."

Unfortunately only three issues of the second volume of the *Gazette* appeared, and in the last number Harvey wrote a poem which was printed with the accompanying message from the men.

"This poem was written to accompany parcels of comforts and cigarettes to us when we were in France, from former members of the Battalion. The author was one of these and is now happy in again bearing arms with Gloucestershire men in the Home Guard."

When war was declared Harvey had announced, "Patrick and I will shoulder our rifles," and when Mr Anthony Eden, the Secretary of State for War, called for the Local Defence Volunteers in 1940 to repel the threatened invasion, Harvey was one of the first in the village to go forward. In fact, there were only two or three rifles between the whole company and it was typical of the Foresters that at the beginning, lacking any other weapon, they took pikes to defend themselves. It was not until the formation of the official Home Guard that they became better equipped.

Frequently before taking his turn at guard duty, Harvey would call in at the local mission church to pray, and when his duty was over he and his companion would repair to the nearest pub to quench their thirst.

A letter from Harvey on the subject of the Home Guard appeared in the Autumn 1941 issue of the *Fifth Glo'ster Gazette*:

"Dear Gloucesters,
These few lines from an old comrade who thinks you may be

interested in (and amused by) our H.G., which I joined a few minutes after Mr. Eden's wireless call, thus becoming local 'parashot' No. 1. For so the Press then christened us. L.D.V. (a better name) came later, and to observe how that baby has grown into 'Home Guard' (the most fitting name) is like reading Wells's novel *Food of the Gods* wherein jam-eating wasps developed into death-dealing hornets. For the H.G. now numbers more than a million and a half armed men. . . .

"*Our* patrolling is, of course, peculiar to the place, and must be very different from that outside the Forest of Dean. Hence my praise of that poacher who knows every woodland track, rack and ride; he of whom I have heard that he had 'shot everything on the hill, and netted everything but the north wind.' Heaven help any Jerries found wandering over *his* preserves!

"Yet I feel that in their shoes I might be grateful to fall into H.G. hands rather than into those of certain wives who upon times follow or accompany their men. Surely from no jealous or suspicious motives, but rather with a desire to 'shove a hot poker down the neck of *that wicked man* handle fust!' Asked why 'handle fust' the wife in question replied, 'So as 'im 'ud burn his hands off trying to get it out on 'im!' "

During the first few years of the war Harvey contributed intermittently to radio programmes and to the local papers. His legal cases were dwindling, though he was often called in by other solicitors to act as a Commissioner for Oaths, when he would walk in to Lydney from Yorkley, glad to earn five shillings a time.

In 1943 his mother died and this had a profound effect upon him. After she had a stroke he could not bring himself to go and see her; he preferred to remember her as she had been before and his family had great difficulty in persuading him to go to her funeral. He had long seemed to have had the feeling that he had let her down in some way and had been a disappointment to her. When he realised that she would no longer be there in the background of his life, he felt like a ship without a rudder.

> How could I guess until this hour that she —
> Whose influence more permanent had been
> Than timeless things; than all that I had seen,
> Or heard, or felt, since first I came to be:
> She whom, if seeing not, I knew was there,
> Some miles or score of miles away at home —
> Would find a dwelling where I might not come
> To touch her hand even, or touch her hair.[1]

---

[1] "The Isle is full of Noises", *Gloucestershire*, Oliver & Boyd 1947 p. 18.

In 1947 the publishers Oliver & Boyd had agreed to produce an anthology of his poems and Mr. T. Hannam-Clark, a Gloucester dignitary, had been approached to write the preface. In a letter to him Harvey wrote (in an extremely shaky, almost illegible hand):

"Many thanks for your welcome and witty letter. Yes, many *are* unpublished and now *all* out of print. You will recognise these latter by a new seriousness . . .

"Living (a rather melancholy Jacques) in the Forest during 30 years of 'Peace' ("a period of cheating between two periods of fighting" — Ambrose Bence, *The Devil's Dick* . . .) has strained, but I hope *not* broken what Masefield wrote of my book *Comrades in Captivity* in two words — 'Courage and Gaiety.' *C in C* is also out of print and I suppose also out of fashion as no-one will re-publish it. It may be some time when I am dead that 'people who like this sort of thing' (and those sorts of virtue) 'will find this the sort of thing they like.'. . ."[1]

The local papers reviewed the book favourably:

"The Gloucestershire Laureate, F.W. Harvey writes with that charm, humour and kindliness which so well befits his native county."[2]

"*Gloucestershire*, (Oliver & Boyd Edinburgh 5/-) a new book of F.W. Harvey's verse, contains his old favourites, together with others that are likewise fresh and simple. It is out of the mainstream of modern verse and is content to present us with charm of colour and plain earthy wit . . ."[3]

Leonard Clark, who had once been offered friendship and help by Harvey, wrote for the *Dean Forest Mercury*,

"Harvey is, of course, the greatest and most native of all Gloucestershire poets. His poems will be remembered as Speech House, Gloucester Cathedral, and the Severn Bore are remembered by those Gloucestershire men who are alone in a strange land. 'Ducks' praised by Chesterton, has already passed into literation. Bridges compared 'Ghosts' with 'The Wife of Usher's Well', while 'The Bugler' is better known in America than in England. Harvey's poems are the true mirror of the man. They are forthright, tender and humorous, as he is forthright, tender and humorous. They spring from a kindly heart and from a deeply religious mind, which has never allowed itself to be seduced by the prevailing poetic fashion. This selection from his poems reveals for us not only the original thoughts and passionate feelings of a genuine countryman, but also unrolls before our eyes, the most exciting map of Gloucestershire, with all its

---

[1] The Gloucester Collection, Gloucester City Library.
[2] Review of *Gloucestershire*, 'Gloucester Echo', 13.1.48.
[3] Review of *Gloucestershire*, 'The Citizen', 25.2.48.

hills, churches, people and pubs . . ."

However, sales of the book were poor and so it was a loss to its publishers and a great disappointment to Harvey. Two years later he wrote an article for the magazine *The Gloucestershire Countryside* entitled 'The Poet and the Public' in which he tried to analyse the reasons for the decline in the popularity of poetry and he ended with these words:

"Somebody, this is the plain fact, must somehow or other convince the public that poetry can and does comprehend normal joys of normal beings. Then books of verse may again be among the best sellers, and why should they not be? Then their production will no longer be what it is today, a class — nay worse — a money privilege. Then also will poetry be what by right it is — the joy of common men, not the little superiority of cliques."[1]

The satirical work of G.K. Chesterton appealed to Harvey and when a doctor friend expressed an interest in these poems, Harvey cut a page out of Chesterton's *Songs of Education* and sent them to him to read. About the same time he was asked by a cousin to recommend something to read, and again he suggested Chesterton, saying,

". . . the G.K.C. prescription is, like many of us, rather the worse for wear, but not copyright and so if you like you could get it typed in duplicate and keep a clean copy, sending me another if you possess or control the typing tools, which I do not.

"In any case please return all originals, script, cuttings, letter etc. as I have no more.

"Hoping you and maybe others of the family will like the taste and with love and good wishes to All
Will."[2]

Harvey must have also enclosed the script of his 1927 talk to the Gloucester Rotarians on Chesterton together with a cutting of the report from the local paper.

As Harvey's periods of work became more sporadic, so his financial problems grew and his appeals to relations and friends to help him out of his difficulties became more frequent. He always intended to pay back the loans, but was seldom in a position to do so. He had never had any idea how to handle money; no-one was able to get an account from

---

[1] 'The Poet and the Public', F.W. Harvey, *The Gloucestershire Countryside*, Vol. 6 No. 10, Jan-Mar 1949, p. 197.
[2] Letter from F.W.H. to Mr. Cecil Watts.

F. W. HARVEY,
SOLICITOR.

LYDNEY,

GLOS.

To:- Our Dear Cousin Louise.

Greetings, & Know All Men by these Presents:
That Our said beloved cousin is hereby
Enjoined and Commanded to appear
in Person again to reign over her
subjects (& bully all if so it be required)
without any undue delay, whether of
Doctor or Matron or Nurse, & from henceforward
never again to associate with Surgeons
or Hospitals; but to enjoy the Majesty
of Weather provided for her in her Realm
in this time of Spring & the Cuckoo.
Signed George Rex ● ● ●
by hand of his faithful minstrel
of hand & tone

F. W. HARVEY.

= (Cousin Will.)

April 20th in the year of our Lord
1949

A letter written by Will to his cousin Louise on her being discharged from hospital.
By courtesy of Mr Melville Watts

A postcard from Harvey written to the author by candlelight and accidentally caught in the flame.

him and his own bills were always overlooked. He had never believed in saving or hoarding and so relied on luck and good fortune to carry him through life. His own generosity prompted the same feeling in others, who tried to help him financially or in kind. As Mr. F.W. Baty wrote in an appreciation of Harvey:

"F.W. was, above all, an honest man, he had faced a hard, material world and knew that he was beaten.

"I realised the harshness of that beating when, in exchange for permission to use one of his poems, he asked only for a gallon or two of paraffin for his stove...

"Our last meeting was in a bar overlooking Westbury churchyard. Lifting his pint he turned to the window and gave a toast — 'To some of my good friends, till we meet again'."[1]

Although he was in no position to do so, he continued to meet his Forest friends daily in the pubs, seeking out their company to lift his spirits.

One of his favourite forms of amusement was to meet together with a friend in the Bailey Inn to play what they called the 'Village Idiot' game. As each of them took little interest in his appearance and could speak the Forest dialect, it was not difficult to fool any unsuspecting 'foreigner' who might enter the pub for a drink.

His unconventional mode of living was affecting his health. He would not be confined by regular times for taking meals, but would often carry an egg and a lemon in his pocket, stopping somewhere on his way to ask for the loan of a lemon squeezer and a glass. It was probably this lack of interest in food which led to his final illness, for while he was never particularly interested in eating, he would always happily share a drink with anyone, as this presented the opportunity for conversation and companionship.

He took to going for walks through the village morning and evening, his head bowed in meditation. He never kept a dog as a companion, but he was often followed by the half dozen or so geese which wandered freely in his garden.

For years Harvey had been a member of the British Legion and had been made President of his local branch, so it was he who laid the wreath on the war memorial at the Remembrance Day service. Brian Waters was once present at this ceremony and described his impressions of it in a chapter of his book *The Forest of Dean*.[2]

---

[1] Appreciation of F.W.H. written for the occasion of the dedication of a plaque in his memory by F.W. Baty, 1980.
[2] *The Forest of Dean*, Brian Waters, 1951, Chap. XV.

"It was Remembrance Day and the foresters were trickling towards the war memorial, a simple cenotaph on the sward among the oaks. . . . A little phalanx stood on the sward, young men and a shingling of older ones — the survivors of two wars. Seated apart from them with the poppy wreath of the British Legion in his hand sat the poet, not by right of his poetry but because he is the leading fighting man of the village. I have always hitherto met him face to face in the brisk companionship of friendship, but today, sitting in his isolation, I view him with detachment for the first time. I see him in profile, and the silhouette of that sensitive, genial face is that of a fighter who won the D.C.M. for a feat of bravery more in keeping with the spirit of the Homeric age than modern warfare. . . .

"Today a small elderly man, he sits thinking, I am sure, of those comrades of his youth who have been spared the bitter knowledge of another war."

When the book was published in 1951 Harvey wrote a letter to the editor of the local paper:

"Sir, — Mr. Brian Waters has written a fine book on The Forest of Dean.

"It contains many kind references to myself which I am loath to discourage in an age more notable for spiteful exchanges between fellow authors.

"But I cannot permit him to write that I laid the British Legion wreath upon the cenotaph because I was the best fighting man of the village.

"That honour was accorded me because I happened to be President of the local Legion Branch.

"I hold that all soldiers who tried bravely to do their duty, (whether decorated or not) are equal — there can be no 'best' among them.

"Thanking you therefore, Brian, for your generous praise, but disclaiming this item.

"Your sincere admirer and friend,
F.W. Harvey

P.S. On review I find the word used was 'leading' not 'best' but the disclaimer still stands. — F.W.H."[1]

In January 1956 Harvey was the subject of a radio portrait for a monthly programme of the Arts in the West Country, entitled

---

[1] Harvey's Scrapbook, Gloucester County Record Office.

'Signature'. It was devised by Charles Brewer, himself a Gloucester man, son of Sir Herbert Brewer, the cathedral organist. In a short introductory article in the *Radio Times*, Brewer wrote:

"Few, if any, established poets capable of the profound sincerity and imaginative approach which shines forth from all his serious verse can at the same time equal his delicious sense of the comic in his lighter work. All that has flowed from his pen . . . is a joyful hymn of praise to the Creator for all that beauty of nature which lies unfolded between the Cotswolds and the Welsh Border . . ."[1]

Of the broadcast the correspondent of the *Dean Forest Mercury* wrote:

"The broadcast script shows how faithfully has been grasped the philosophy and the genius of the man who has a wholesome love of his native soil — his beloved Gloucestershire. It showed that Harvey has done for Gloucestershire what Housman did for Shropshire."

In September 1956 Harvey was asked to write the report of the performance of 'The Dream of Gerontius' at the Three Choirs Festival. He wrote an urgent appeal to some friends in Gloucester to put him up for the night.

"I am told to 'cover' the 'Dream of Gerontius' for a Forest paper on Tuesday next and have consented for joy of the work. But I have no means of getting home that night. (What a pity Mother is not living at Minsterworth instead of Heaven!) Can you for one night and sake of old times, *put me up* — or 'up with me'? Please reply by return and if so where and when we meet in late afternoon.

Affectionately yrs.

Will Harvey."[2]

His friends gladly granted his request and after the performance talked far into the night. He read his poems to them with great gusto and showed some wonderful flashes of the old Harvey whom they had known in the past.

He already knew his days were numbered and had no fear. He said he felt he had done *some* things in life of which he could be proud. He confessed that he had already written the outline of his 'write-up' in advance and when he returned home he wrote a letter of thanks to his friends (on the back of a circular letter received by him!) and clipped to it with a hairgrip were cuttings from the papers.

---

[1] 'Sing a Song of Gloucestershire' *Radio Times* January 1956.
[2] Letter from F.W.H. to Mr Brian Frith.

"You may care to see the enclosed press cuttings — if only to note the relative space allotted to each! But I write to thank you *all* very much for your welcome last Tuesday. I shall think of you when blowing my nose (which is *very often!*) as, believe me, in my prayers, I always do.

F.W.H."[1]

The cuttings were the coverage of the 'Dream of Gerontius' and the report of a case (which Harvey lost) of a man accused of driving while under the influence of drink.

The reference to blowing his nose was occasioned by his hosts having lent him a handkerchief as he had a heavy cold and had forgotten, or lost his own.

The last words of his report were, 'The theme is commonplace and stupendous. You reader and I are (or shall be) quite personally involved, for the theme is no less than Death and the Hereafter...'

A few weeks later Harvey lay seriously ill. Eventually he had to be taken to hospital, but when it was discovered that nothing could be done for him, he was sent home to be nursed by his wife.

During his last days many of his relations and old friends went to visit him, and grieved to see him suffering. He remained lucid to the end, quoting Housman. His final words were,

"I am burnt out to the glory of Gloucestershire."

He died on 13th February 1957 and although a Roman Catholic, he was buried in the family grave at Minsterworth. The coffin, draped with the Union Jack, was taken from the church past a guard of honour formed by the British Legion. The brimful Severn less than a hundred yards away, shone in the winter sun and suddenly across the meadows came a peal of bells from a neighbouring church. Two of his poems were read over the grave and then he was buried beside a hundred year old yew tree, facing an apple orchard.

The headstone on the grave bears the inscription

Frederick William Harvey D.C.M.
Soldier and Poet
Born 26.3.88
Died 13.2.57
A Gloucestershire Lad

There is no epitaph, but one of his poems could well have served:

---

[1] Letter from F.W.H. to Mr. Brian Frith.

O Lord, within my heart for ever,
Set this sweet shape of land and winding river,
That I may taste their comfort till I die
And feed upon them in Eternity.[1]

In fact, in a fifteen minute radio talk on 'Epitaphs' nearly thirteen years earlier, he claimed to have written his own, perhaps with his tongue in his cheek:

"Not many men write their own memorials, but some do. For instance I have. It's contained in five words which you can take in any way you like. I should like to be buried in my own parish church where my mother and father are lying, and the bloom blows over the wall from a nearby orchard. And I should like a granite tombstone — marble doesn't wear well in this hostile climate of ours, and on that tombstone I should like inscribed the five words,

And the same to you"[2]

Long obituaries appeared in the local papers. In the *Lydney Observer* it was said,

"One of his colleagues once said to the writer of this tribute 'Harvey's honest, straight as a die'."

Brian Waters writing in *The Citizen* and *The Gloucestershire Countryside* said of him:

"With the death of F.W. Harvey, Gloucestershire has said farewell to its greatest writer and this county's most outstanding poet...

"... Though humour was very strong in Harvey, his humanity saved his poetry from the triviality of light verse. Above all it is entertaining and demands to be read aloud, and this is a true test of merit."

The *Times'* obituary said:

"In several unforgettable lyrics his poetry has evoked the scenery and atmosphere of Gloucestershire, and his dialect poems have captured not only the accent but the idiom of his native speech."

Leonard Clark, in an appreciation wrote:

"Will Harvey is dead and my heart is struck with sorrow. With anger too, that the literary critics did not give him the encouragement he so badly needed 30 years ago, nor recognise his true poetic worth."

In December 1958 the B.B.C. created a sound portrait of Harvey

---

[1] "A Prayer", *Gloucestershire*, Oliver & Boyd, 1947, p. 35.
[2] "Here Lies...", B.B.C. Home Service, June 1944 — Harvey's Scrapbook, Gloucester County Record Office.

drawn by the voices of those who had known him, and one of these, Brian Waters, said that although Harvey's work had been confined to a few years of high productivity, nevertheless the poet had once remarked to him,

"My whole life has been a poem."

Today three of his poems are listed in Granger's *Index to Poetry*, four more appeared in the second volume of a series of books entitled *Poet's England* and his poem "November" was selected for inclusion in *The Oxford Book of Twentieth Century Verse*. After he died a selection of his unpublished poems were collected together by Mr. Frank Green of Lydney in a small duplicated pamphlet under the title *A Forest Offering*. In his review of it Leonard Clark wrote:

"... he had, to the end, a very individual 'knobbly' way of saying things which could bring tears to the heart. Harvey was always a skilled versifier who knew how to handle rhyme and rhythm."

Finally, in 1983 a further small collection of his poems was published under the title *Collected Poems 1912-1957*. In the Introduction Brian Frith wrote:

"... for those who do not yet know his poems, and who love this county, there are treasures awaiting them from one who gave so much and received so little."

In speaking of himself Harvey had once said:

"I know I am an artist, but a small artist not a great one. Whatever I have written has always been sincere, however badly expressed. Whatever I have given to others through my poetry, I am only returning what God has given to me."

Harvey's message was that man is formed not only of body and mind, but above all of spirit and this was the most important thing to him, which came out strongly in much of his poetry. His friend, Brian Waters, once expressed the hope that,

"Some day, it may be tomorrow or it may be centuries hence, the world will discover what a fine poet Will Harvey really is."[1]

In March 1980, twenty-three years after his death, his worth was finally recognised when a slate memorial tablet was placed on the South Transept wall of Gloucester Cathedral inscribed with these words:

Frederick William Harvey D.C.M.
Soldier and Poet of Gloucestershire
1888-1957
"He loved the vision of this world and found it good"

---

[1] "F.W. Harvey: Poet of the Dean", Brian Waters, *The Gloucestershire Countryside* July-September 1948.

Bibliography

Gloucestershire Friends 1917.   F.W. Harvey.   Sidgwick & Jackson.

A Gloucestershire Lad 1918.   F.W. Harvey.   Sidgwick & Jackson.

Ducks & Other Verses 1919.   F.W. Harvey.   Sidgwick & Jackson.

Comrades in Captivity 1920.   F.W. Harvey.   Sidgwick & Jackson.

Farewell 1921.   F.W. Harvey.   Sidgwick & Jackson.

September & Other Poems 1925.   F.W. Harvey.   Sidgwick & Jackson.

*The Augustan Books of English
   Poetry* 1926.   F.W. Harvey.   *Editor*   Humbert Wolfe

A Forest Offering.   F.W. Harvey.   Frank Green.

Gloucestershire 1947.   F.W. Harvey.   Oliver & Boyd.

In Pillowell Woods 1926.   F.W. Harvey.   Frank H. Harris.

Collected Poems 1983.   F.W. Harvey.   Douglas McLean.

*A Glossary of the Cotswold
   (Gloucestershire) Dialect* 1868.   Rev.R.W.   Huntley.

*A Glossary of Dialect & Archaic words
   used in the County of Gloucestershire* 1890.   J. Drummond Robertson

The Forest of Dean 1952.   F.W. Baty.   Regional Books (R. Hale).

A Look at Lydney.   John Powell.

The Forest of Dean 1951.   Brian Waters.   Chequer Press.

A Child in the Forest 1974.   Winifred Foley.   B.B.C.

A Fool in the Forest 1965.   Leonard Clark.   Dennis Dobson.

The Ordeal of Ivor Gurney 1978.   Michael Hurd.   O.U.P.

Other Sources

The Fifth Glo'ster Gazette 1915-1918 and Vol. 2 Nos 1 & 3 1939.
The Gloucestershire Countryside July-Sept 1948 and Jan-Mar 1949.
The Listener Dec 12th 1957.
The Radio Times Jan 18th 1956.
The Gloucester Journal.
The Gloucester Echo.
The Citizen.
The Lydney Observer.
The Dean Forest Mercury.
The Times Literary Supplement.
The Morning Post Oct 3rd 1915.
The County Record Office Gwent.
The Gurney Archive, Gloucester City Library.
Letters from F.W.H. to Mr. Brian Frith, Mr. T. Hannam-Clark,
    Mr. Cecil Watts.
Copy of typescript of B.B.C. broadcast Dec 8th 1958.
Harvey's Scrapbook, County Record Office, Gloucester.
A W.I. Scrapbook — Minsterworth 1850-1951. The Gloucester
    Collection, Gloucester City Library.